African Grey Parro

African Grey Parrot Owner's Manual

African Grey Parrot care, interaction, feeding, training and common mistakes

by

Martin Monderdale

Table of Contents

Chapter 1) Introduction

I absolutely love the African Grey Parrot, but looking back, I probably wasn't ready to own one when I first got one. I liked the idea of a parrot who could talk to me. I also didn't have a yard for a dog and I didn't want an inside dog or cat. The parrot was therefore the best choice.

This is certainly a pet that takes time to get to know. It takes time to care for each day too. You will need to be able to offer it a connection that it would otherwise get in the wild. By instinct, these parrots are part of a flock. When you own one as a pet, you become their flock.

I don't regret owning these beloved parrots by any means. I do feel guilty at times though, because I don't think the first ones I had got the best care they should have. Now I know the best practices and I feel confident that I can care for them like I should.

The first ones I had actually belonged to my grandmother. She asked me to care for them when she no longer could. They adored her and I always felt they missed her. Knowing all I do about these birds now, I realize the bond she had with them was very deep. I was able to care for them, but they never bonded with me in the same way.

The African Grey Parrot requires plenty of care. Don't assume that getting a bird will reduce the amount of care you give your pet. They need to be challenged mentally and they need to socialize. They need to be fed and you need to learn about their behaviors. If you don't take care of them like you should, negative behaviors often result.

I am excited to share with you what it takes to really take care of African Grey Parrots as pets. If you can't completely commit to such needs, this isn't the right pet for you. Don't get one because you think they are cool or you enjoy pirate movies! Get one because you are ready to bond with one of the most exceptional creatures out there.

There is no doubt in my mind that this is one of the most talented bird species out there! They have a great reputation but each African Grey Parrot has their own personality and behavior. Training them early shows them who is in charge and what to expect. Be firm with the rules so they are willing to follow them.

It is amazing just how intelligent these birds are. They have been kept as pets since Biblical times. They were respected for their beauty and for their brilliance. They continue to be popular today due to the bond they have with their owner, their desire to learn, and the fact that many of us (including me) are completely in awe of them!

The African Grey Parrot is classified as a medium sized bird. That information will come in handy if you decide to get one as a pet. You will need to get the right size cage and the right perches for your pet. They are light grey in color and feature a crimson tail.

The eyes are orange and they are often mistaken at a distance for pigeons. When you look at them up close, you will see they have a plumage featuring a scalloped pattern. The plumage looks like they are wearing an armored suit. The seashell-like design is laid across the body, touching each other with some overlay.

Be prepared to stay on your toes if you have an African Grey Parrot as a pet. They are excellent companions. I enjoy mine very much. If you live alone they are the ideal pet because you will feel like you have someone to talk to all the time. In a busy household, you must make sure you allocate enough time to your parrot.

Just like each person has a different level of intelligence, you will discover that with these parrots too. Don't get one and then force it to learn 1,500 words just because they are able to. If you encourage ongoing learning with your parrot through proper training techniques they can learn plenty. You can't force them though and you need to avoid getting frustrated.

Don't get into a race with others who own such a bird. As long as yours is happy and healthy, that is all that matters. What often occurs though is people see videos or read a book with an owner and their parrot interacting and it is above what they have going on in their own house. Then they feel inadequate, but that shouldn't be the case at all.

I love my African Grey Parrots being able to talk and say various words. But I will admit it is the fact they can speak in different voices that really amuses me. Sometimes, one of them sounds just like my wife! The first few times, it freaked me out a bit. Yet it isn't out of the ordinary for them to sound like one of their owners.

Sometimes, one of our African Grey Parrots will bark like the dog or meow like the cat. It has even been known to call the cat! They are able to imitate sounds and make a thud like the sliding glass door closing or opening. It is just mind blowing sometimes all they can learn.

They don't just mimic either; they are able to use what they learn. Seeing your parrot being intelligent, learning, and vocalizing what it has learned is a fascinating experience. When I train my African Grey Parrots, I am as proud as a parent of a toddler learning new words and new things.

These birds tend to be one person oriented. The person that socializes with them the most is who they are prone to stick with. My wife loves these birds as much as I do, and we have enjoyed training them together over the years. Some have preferred her to me and with others it has been in my corner. Be ready to make a lifetime commitment to your parrot if you decide this is a good pet for you.

When they are properly cared for, they can live up to 50 years. The first two I had were adopted and I am not sure how old they were when I got them. The one we have now was purchased very young and it just may outlive me!

These aren't low cost pets either, so keep that in mind. You can buy African Grey Parrots starting around $600 but some can be up to $2,000. It depends on where you buy them and other factors. We will cover that in depth in an upcoming chapter.

Be well aware of who you buy them from and what they have to offer. Don't buy them from people you don't know. It should always be on your mind why they are selling such a delightful bird. I recommend buying a youngster but there are some wonderful adult African Grey Parrots in need of a home too.

You can keep these pets in an apartment, a house, and other dwellings. They do make noise but usually it won't be enough to bother your neighbors. The exception is a parrot that isn't getting enough attention. It is very likely to start screaming.

It is important to keep their cage clean and to offer them plenty of toys for interaction. That will keep them stimulated while you can't be with them. They do need daily interaction, so if you will be gone, make sure you have someone you can trust to take care of your parrot.

My wife and I go on vacation once a week and a neighbor comes over to care for ours. The parrot is familiar with this person and recognizes their voice. While he isn't crazy about her in terms of wanting to really interact with her, he isn't stressed or nervous around her either. If you plan to have someone care for your African Grey Parrot, make sure the two are familiar with each other before you go.

There is a great deal of decision making that should factor into the equation before you buy this type of pet. It goes well beyond just being able to afford it. The commitment to daily care is very important. Knowing your parrot is essential to identify any changes in health or behavior immediately.

In future chapters, you will discover the various needs African Grey Parrots have. I hope you will use that information to help you decide if this is a good pet for you. If it is, I encourage you to take your time finding the right place to buy it. I also encourage you to continue learning about your parrot so you can make the environment one it thrives in.

If you decide this isn't the right pet for you, don't be disappointed. It is far better to have explored the idea and decided against it than to blindly get one as a pet and not be able to care for it well. The truth is these birds aren't right for every household.

If you do decide the African Grey Parrot is going to be a wonderful pet for you, I will tell you it is going to be a thrilling experience. It is going to be a way for you to engage with your pet and to watch them grow and learn. There will be days when you just can't wait to get home from work so you can spend time with your parrot.

There is plenty to learn about this bird before you can decide if it is right for you or not. Take an inventory of what it needs and what you have to offer. Are you willing to make changes to your lifestyle to accommodate their needs? Can you afford the cost of their care on a regular basis?

If you rent rather than own your residence, always talk to your landlord to make sure the bird will be allowed to live there. Some apartments state no birds due to the neighbors. You don't want to buy such a bird, become attached to it, and then either have to get rid of it or break your lease and move in order to keep it.

You may have children or other pets. You may be considering children in the future and wonder how it will work with a parrot like this. We will cover that in a future chapter as well.
When they are well trained and properly cared, for they are going to be an exceptional investment of your money, your time, and you will wonder what you ever did without your African Grey Parrot in your home!

Chapter 2) History and Habitat

You may be curious about these creatures in terms of where they come from and how they became pets. By law, it is illegal for an African Grey Parrot to be taken out of the wild and sold as a pet. Instead, those offered as pets are bred for that sole purpose.

I feel it is important to share with you some of the history and information about the natural habitat, the natural instincts and the ancestral line of the African Grey Parrot.

There are two types of parrots that fall into the category of 'African Grey Parrot'. The Timneh African Grey and the Congo African Grey. The latter has a darker gray color, with the first being more silver. The Congo is also larger in size when fully grown than the Timneh.

History

As mentioned in the previous chapter, there are documented incidents of these parrots in Biblical times. They were prized possessions and believed to be very beautiful. To see one was good luck and those who owned one as a pet were considered to be very fortunate.

Where they came from in order to be captured and then bred in these early times isn't known. It is believed that food was set out for them as traps. There are stories of these parrots being sent to spy and listen to conversations and report back. We know that is likely not true – they do not have that much intellectual power to follow such directions.

Yet it did help to keep people quiet. Servants were believed to avoid gossiping when there were such parrots around. They didn't want to be punished or killed if the bird was to repeat something they had said.

Throughout history, there are references to this parrot as being very beautiful and very majestic. It has always been highly regarded for its intelligence and the ability to repeat words and phrases. Some reports throughout history indicate that some cultures felt there was a link between these birds and death.

There are books dating around 1885 that have to do with caring for the African Grey Parrot. While so little was known about them at the time, the desire to own one was very high.

In Europe, the wealthy enjoyed this parrot due to their beauty and their intelligence. King Henry VII of England had several of them as pets. The pet parrot belonging to Duchess of Lennox, Frances Teresa Stuart, is the oldest taxidermy bird found. It dates back to 1702.

Habitat

The original habitat for both species of African Grey Parrots is very diverse around Africa. Their intelligence allows them to be able to adapt to a variety of surroundings. As long as they are able to find food and shelter they will stick around an area. If need be, they will move on to get their basic needs met.

They are known to reside around:

- Savannas
- Mangroves along the coast
- Woodlands
- Forest edges that have been cleared.

They are mainly found around the Central and Western areas of Africa. The Congo has a wider habitat. They are found residing around Tanzania, Kenya, and the Ivory Coast. The Timneh species isn't naturally found living on those areas.

African Grey Parrots tend to stay in a flock. By the light of the early morning, they will call to each other. They will go out seeking food. Throughout the day they will forage in the trees and find shelter from the heat and predators. At night, they will roost in the trees.

They are able to talk to each other in the wild, but it isn't like what we hear when we walk into the pet store. Instead of words, they have their own sounds and lingo that they use to interact with each other. This will happen if you have two of these parrots together too. They may learn to interact with each other as their flock and not pick up spoken words as well.

In the wild, their diet consists of:

- Nuts
- Seeds
- Fruit
- Leaves

In the wild, they tend to live about 25 years. That is half the estimated time span for one in good health, which is well cared for in captivity. They are mature and able to mate around 4 or 5 years of age.

In the wild, African Grey Parrots are exposed to harsh conditions, predators, limited food supplies at times, and stress. All of this can significantly impact their life span. Yet they tend to do well in the wild because they are intelligent and they can problem solve.

They remember where food sources are, even those that are seasonal. They are very intuitive and that helps them to thrive in a variety of environments. There has been plenty of research over the years on these parrots. Some of the in depth studies have been done by Dr. Irene Pepperberg. She has worked with these delightful birds since the 1970s.

Her work is fascinating, and I encourage you to explore what she has done with them. She once had a parrot that was able to recite the alphabet and count to six. He was also able to successfully identify many objects when he was shown photos of them.

Pepperberg has noted in her studies about African Grey Parrots being able to process information and make choices based on the information they have. They are able to learn concepts and to problem solve. It is very interesting to read about all of the observations she has made about their level of intelligence.

What is so important about such research spanning several decades is it disclaims critics who feel they only mimic what they are taught. While African Grey Parrots will mimic, that is just the tip of the iceberg about how their brains work and how they can function.

Her studies also show that not all of these parrots are as vocal as others. It is the same with humans! We all know those friends who barely uphold their end of the conversation. Yet we know they are very intelligent and there is plenty going on in that brain of theirs.

We also have that friend who never stops talking. Some of these birds will repeat everything they hear! This includes the TV, the doorbell, other pets you may have, and even conversations you have with your family or friends. I used to make smoothies every morning for breakfast. It didn't surprise me when one of the African Grey Parrots I had as a pet started mimicking blender sounds!

Her research also verifies that these parrots can be both curious and mischievous. This can result in some unique situations – both in the wild and in captivity. There is evidence to suggest these parrots do have a sense of humor and they are capable of playing pranks.

You may not believe it until your pet does it – but you have been warned! Some of them are also quite sarcastic. They are able to identify when to be silly, when to be serious, and when to test you. If you don't let this get to you but see it for the phenomenon it is, you can understand the diversity in their personalities.

The African Grey Parrot has been able to survive all this time in the wild and in captivity due to how adaptive they are. They are able to explore, to learn, and to problem solve. They have a great deal of talent and that is evident in their behaviors and their characteristics.

If you ever get the chance to witness them in the wild, it is going to blow you away. They have it made when they are pets, but they are determined to survive and thrive in the wild. They don't rely just on instinct but rather they are able to evolve.

They develop strong bonds in the wild within their flock. When they are in captivity, they do the same with their owner. It helps them to be calm, to focus, and to feel their sensitivity to the fullest. They are capable of strong emotions, and you will see that emerge as you get to know your pet.

When you are sad, they will be sad. Even if you don't tell them what is going on, they are able to pick it up from your voice and your mannerisms. They will do all they can to cheer you up and to help you feel better. They may sing you sweet songs and even rub their head against you affectionately to help express they know how you feel.

Being so sensitive can be a burden on the African Grey Parrot. This is why as an owner, you need to do all you can to provide a loving and relaxing atmosphere. If your home is often filled with tension, this isn't going to be an environment where they can thrive. They can adapt to plenty, but not such dire circumstances.

Chapter 3) Characteristics of the African Grey Parrot

Each of them is very different, but that doesn't mean they don't share similar characteristics. While we can draw somewhat of a picture from what we have observed of African Grey Parrots as a whole, you have to break them down into individuals to fully appreciate what they are all about.

Every single one of them is unique and will develop some characteristics and traits that are their own. Think about children for a moment – you can have several children in the same home with the same parents, yet they all have different characteristics.

If you are going to provide a quality home for the African Grey Parrot, you need to be well aware of their characteristics. You must be patient and you must be attentive or this isn't going to be a good arrangement for either of you. The last thing you want is to resent this pet you have in your home.

Sensitive

I love the fact that these parrots are so sensitive. They can actually tune in to the mood of their owners. This is part of what makes them the most amazing companion birds out there. However, their sensitive nature can also cause them stress or even negative behaviors.

Try to keep the same routine as much as possible for their environment. They are quite intuitive and they will start to pick up on patterns about when you are going to leave for work and when you will get home. If you have a very irregular schedule from one day to the next, it can be hard for them.

The sensitivity issues will be worst when you first take your African Grey Parrot home, but they will eventually adapt.

By understanding their sensitivity issues early on, you will be more prepared when you get your bird home. If they have a meltdown, it doesn't mean you are a bad owner. It just means they need some time to adjust to their new surroundings. In time, your pet will love you and will trust you. Yet that doesn't happen overnight.

You must be patient and build that relationship on a daily basis. As they see you are there to interact with them daily and to feed them daily, they will become attached to you. Even if you are giving the bird 100% of your attention, they are going to be hesitant and withdrawn at first.

Each African Grey Parrot can be different in terms of how much time it takes for them to completely warm to you. Be willing to give them this time, and don't take it personally if they need plenty of it. Think about the relationships you have with others.

Some of them were an instant hit from the start. Others didn't get off to a great start but over time they improved. Most of them started with an introduction and then over time there was trust being built and more interacting. That is what will happen with your African Grey Parrot in time.

Talking

For the most part, these parrots are very talkative. Be ready for that because it can go on all day! They are one of the most talkative pets you will find out there. If you savor the peace and quiet, this is not a pet for you. It can be fun to get them to repeat words and phrases, though.

It can blow you away when they start to say things in response to what is going on around them. This isn't mimicking but rather their intelligence shining through. I know for a fact they are able to understand what is being said to them.

It is usually around 1 year of age when the African Grey Parrot will start to talk a great deal. Of course some start much sooner and others will start much later. There are some that don't talk much, and that can be disappointing if you really want them to.

You can try to train them but you have to respect their personality traits. Just as children all learn differently, so do parrots. The key is to find the way in which they learn. You can't force them to learn but you can make them want to do it!

Intelligence

As I have mentioned, they are very intelligent. This plays a huge role in their behaviors. Don't become impatient with them due to the constant stimulation they need. A bored parrot is one who will become destructive in their environment. Pay attention to what such behaviors are really trying to tell you.

Due to their intelligence, they can be demanding. You have to set boundaries and limits though or they will walk all over you. This is why only someone well versed in how to take care of them should attempt to do so.

It is a good idea to watch videos about the intelligence of them before you get such a bird. If you aren't fully prepared, it can be intimidating and you may not challenge them enough. On the other hand, don't push them so much that they become stressed.

Allow the learning to move along at a pace you both enjoy. If you aren't sure if they are ready for something, try it! If the results aren't encouraging then back off and go back to something else. Move forward in steps rather than making giant leaps.

There are training programs to consider. Most of them are rated for beginners, intermediates, and advanced learning. Paying attention to such labels can help you to get what you need at the right time. When these parrots aren't challenged they can engage in bad behavior because they are bored so don't get sloppy!

Touching

Socializing with your African Grey Parrot is very important. One way to help keep them calm and to bond is through touching. They don't like too much of it though, so limit the physical contact. Pet your bird when you go to interact with it for a moment and then let it be. Some like to have their heads scratched.

You will have to test the waters to find out how much touching your parrot enjoys. Pay attention to their behaviors as you do so. If they seem to be annoyed or stressed, then don't do it as much. If they seem to really enjoy it then you should continue to do it.

What you may discover is your parrot likes to be touched, by only by you or someone in particular in the household. They will tolerate it just fine for that person but not for anyone else. Don't force your parrot to be touched by others if they don't like it. Pay attention to the cues they are giving you.

Gender

A common question is how to distinguish between a male and a female. There are few visual clues, especially for those under 1 ½ years of age. The feathers of females will be gray around the edges. For males, they will be all red or they can have a bit of white along the edges. If it is important to you to have a particular gender, ask for a DNA test to be done on younger birds before you buy them.

Chapter 4) Is this pet right for you?

While everything I share with you in these materials can help you decide if this is the right pet for you or not, this chapter is important to make you question yourself. You need to know if you can handle the daily, ongoing needs of an African Grey Parrot. This bird isn't right for everyone. I will be the first to admit, I wasn't ready when I got my first one.

I was impressed by their beauty and their intelligence. I didn't look beyond that. I feel guilty now that I reflect back on it. My beloved birds deserved so much more than they got. Sure, they were fed and cared for but I was impatient at times. I didn't realize what was causing bad behaviors. The more you know, the easier it is to decide if you should get one or not.

It also prepares you for the possible trials that can occur. I believe there is always far more value in having a remarkable pet than what you put into it. The rewards stay in your heart and the memories can last a lifetime. Putting your pet first is very important. If you are self-centered or you just have too much on your plate day after day, this pet is going to cause you too much stress.

They will also suffer a great deal of stress and frustration. It is selfish to get an African Grey Parrot just to satisfy your desire to have one. If you can't say you can meet their needs every single day then you should be respectful enough not to bring one home!

In no way am I trying to discourage you, I just want you to be realistic. I want you to think about the welfare of your pet and what it means to properly care for them. I want you to realize this is a very unique pet and therefore it needs specialized care.

When the connection is there and the care is there, nothing will stop the terrific bond that develops. While these birds are very intelligent, they are also very sensitive. Without the right care, they will suffer both physically and emotionally. They can develop behavioral problems, health problems, and their lifespan will be much shorter. That isn't the kind of scenario you want to offer them.

It is no joke when an African Grey Parrot is extremely upset due to their needs not being met. They can scream, they may start to bite, and it can cause self-mutilation. You may come home and wonder what is going on – why is your pet acting crazy? The realization is that your lack of proper care has created that outcome.

Patience

Are you a patient person? It takes a great deal of patience and a wonderful sense of humor to do well with one of these parrots. If you have children, they will learn and grow. They will be your pride and job most of the time. Yet there will be times when they test you and your boundaries.

With an African Grey Parrot, it is like raising a very intelligent kindergartener for decades! They are curious, they can throw tantrums, they can show favoritism towards household members, and they need constant stimulation. If you are getting tired or stressed just thinking about it, don't get such a bird as a pet. You need a very lazy and independent cat instead!

I will be the first to admit, having an African Grey Parrot is going to get you attention. People will think you have the coolest pet around. Your neighbors, friends, family, and co-workers will all want to come to your home to see this pet up close and personal.

Major Differences

The major difference with this type of pet and a dog or a cat is the socialization. Sure, your dog wants to be petted, to play fetch, and to go for a walk. Yet they are content and do well for long hours on their own. Most cats want food, water, and a tummy rub now and then. They can be content for days on their own.

With an African Grey Parrot, they need to have lots and lots of your attention every single day. You need to think of this pet as an extension of yourself and a complete part of your family. As your bird gets settled and accustomed to the surroundings, they will try to take over and dominate.

They are vocal too, most of them anyway. If you get tired of hearing a friend or co-worker chatter all day this bird will make you crazy. If you get tired of dealing with kids talking all day and wish for some peace and quiet, are you sure you want this bird around?

They are going to mimic what they hear, both words and sounds around your household. They are also going to be able to use their intelligence to piece together what to say and when to make certain sounds. I find it amusing but there are people out there that find it annoying. Know your limits and if they are compatible with this parrot before you get one as a pet.

Asthma and Allergies

If anyone in your household suffers from asthma or allergies, don't get an African Grey Parrot. They have plumage, which is very dusty. It makes a hell of a mess for you to clean up after. It also gets allergens circulating in the air. I had a girlfriend for a short period of time when I had my first parrot. She had difficulty breathing just being in my apartment with the bird due to her asthma.

Chewing

Some people can't stand to listen to other people chew their food. They don't like to hear a dog doing it. Well, an African Grey Parrot is going to chew all the time too. They do this as part of their behavior, so don't think you can change it.

Their beak continues to grow all the time. Chewing helps them to keep their beak the right length. If it becomes too long, it is in the way when trying to eat. You must give them plenty of toys to stimulate them and for them to chew on. If you don't, they will chew on anything they can get. This includes their cage, paper you put in the cage, etc.

First Time Bird Owners

As I mentioned previously, the African Grey Parrot isn't recommended for a first time bird owner. There are other birds out there much easier to care for. Yes, I agree, they aren't as lovely and not as intelligent. Yet it can give you a chance to gain confidence and to learn what daily care for a bird is all about.

If your heart and your mind are set on getting nothing else, just make sure you have all the information you need. Buy the bird from someone who can be available to help you, should you have questions or concerns. Take all of this material and apply it. Read it more than once so it sticks with you.

Make friends with other people who own this type of pet. You can share information with each other. You can share your struggles as well as your triumphs. They don't have to be people locally either. You can join various online forums for owners of African Grey Parrots. You will gain a wealth of information, a support system, and make some great friends.

Flock Ideals

According to the experts, part of the reason why African Grey Parrots need to have so much interaction is that they are flock oriented. This is a survival instinct for them in the wild. This accounts for why your pet wants your attention all the time. If you find you can't spend as much time as you need to with your parrot, you may need to get a second one.

By doing so, they will have a mate they can bond with around the clock. Don't expect them to instantly be friends though. They will have to determine their dominance order. You can keep them in separate cages but keep them where they can see and hear each other. This can do wonders for their socialization needs. However, this isn't a replacement for you interacting with them.

They aren't going to do well with other bird species in your home. A flock of birds isn't going to mix – they have to be the same species to live in harmony.

Cuddling

If you want a pet you can cuddle with, this isn't it. As mentioned before, most African Grey Parrots will tolerate some touching now and then. They like to be scratched on the head. They will become impatient and agitated with too much physical interaction with you. There are birds out there that enjoy cuddling, such as Cockatoos.

Chapter 5) Children and Other Pets

If you have children or other pets in your home, you need to think about how bringing an African Grey Parrot into the mix is going to work out. Even if you are fine with it, will they all mix well? Will your kids feel like they don't get enough attention due to the bird? Will the bird feel like it gets enough of your time? Are you going to feel like there isn't enough of you to go around?

These are all questions to think about. It doesn't mean your bird won't like your kids or the other way around. It doesn't mean your bird won't do fine in a household with a dog or a cat. You just have to be ready for anything!

Children

Your children may do very well with your new pet, or they may be jealous of it. With small children, you have to make sure they don't access the parrot without you being around. You also have to make sure they don't stick items into the cage. I have caught my toddler trying to give my African Grey Parrot crayons before!

Never allow children to handle your parrot without an adult right there with them. You don't want any type of accident to occur. Pay attention to the behavior of your bird too. If they get nervous or they feel they are in danger, they may bite. That can be very traumatic for a child.

Children shouldn't be able to reach the latches on the cage to let the bird out. They may think it is fun to do so and that can cause all kinds of chaos in your home. You also have to be careful about what children will teach an African Grey Parrot. It may be funny when they teach it to talk like a pirate at first, but do you want to hear that all the time?

Most experts believe it is good for children to be in a home with at least one pet. It helps to teach them about responsibility. I like the fact that our bird is safely in the cage. He has been kicked a time or two by accident. He simply got in the way when one of the kids was walking around.

If you have children under the age of 12, you need to really think first before getting such a pet. The truth is, children can make these birds very nervous and stressed. In our case, we had the bird first and the babies came later. I am thankful my parrot was fine with the changes. However, I know other owners who didn't have the same results.

African Grey Parrots can and will bite. They can be scary to a child if they try to bite them. Small fingers fit very easily into the space between bars on the cage. As a result, the bird may feel threatened and bite them. Make sure you teach children in your household and visitors to never stick their fingers in there.

Other Pets

I have a dog, and it does well with my parrot. Actually, the parrot was mine and the dog belonged to my wife. So we blended them as best we could. It wasn't always easy for sure. My parrot wanted to let that dog know who was boss! He also mimicked the dog barking. It would confuse the dog and get him all wound up.

Sadly, I have known people with African Grey Parrots who have lost them due to dogs or cats in the home. They killed their beloved bird. If you have more than one pet in your home, you have to take safeguards. You have to make sure the other pets can't get the cage open or knock it over.

You also have to make sure you take care when you let your parrot fly around the house. We always put the dog in the yard before we let the parrot fly around and play a bit. If it is too cold for the dog to go out, we move the parrot to the bedroom and lock the door before we let him out for a bit of flight time.

The fact that your bird and other pets will be home alone at times without supervision can be a concern. You need to make sure the cage is in a location where it can't be accidentally knocked over by a dog or a cat.

Every parrot will be different and when my friend had a puppy, the parrot and the puppy used to like each other and they never had a problem. However, just to be on the safe side, once the puppy grew older, they always had her on a lead when their parrot was out of the cage.

Neighbors

Think about where you live too, if you want to keep the peace. Your parrot isn't going to be quiet. While it isn't going to keep the neighbors up all night all the time, it can create issues. If you have gone to work and your bird starts to scream, is it going to make the lady across the hallway at the apartment complex very upset?

There is no denying these birds can make a great deal of noise at any point in time. If you live in a house, there is very little chance your neighbors are going to hear it. If you live in close proximity to other people, it could be a problem. This is definitely something to think about before you buy an African Grey Parrot.

Can you often hear the neighbors talking or fighting? Do you hear their TV at times? If the answer is yes, there is a good chance the walls are thin. That can also increase the chances of your parrot bothering others around you.

Chapter 6) Meeting their basic needs

Should you decide you would like to have an African Grey Parrot, you must be able to meet their basic needs. This includes the right housing, food, interactions, health care, and more. Are you up for the task? If you are, it is an amazing experience you will love!

However, you must meet their basic needs day after day. If you don't, they are going to rebel and it is going to be hard to get their behavior under control. It is also going to be difficult to keep them happy. These birds can suffer from depression if they aren't interacting enough with you.

They can start to destroy their living areas in the cage if you aren't keeping them mentally stimulated. African Grey Parrots love to keep busy and they need to be able to enjoy a lifestyle that has plenty of routine in it.

If they learn early on that you will return after you have been gone for a period of time, they aren't going to be stressed or upset. They will learn that it is part of the routine for them to engage in.

When you are home you need to make sure you do interact with them often. There are plenty of puzzles and toys you can give them to keep them busy during the day but in the end they will crave your presence and your attention.

If you like to have your thoughts to yourself after a day at work, this isn't the right pet for you. They are going to be ready for your attention as soon as you walk in the door. You have to be ready for it and to not be resentful to them for it.

Flight Time and Safety

At the core of meeting the basic needs of your bird is the issue of overall safety. You have to balance fun and interacting with them along with the need for safety. Survey your environment and think about what could happen if they got out or how they could be in danger.

We will talk more about housing for these birds in a later chapter. However, the cages need to be at least 34 inches wide and 34 inches deep. You can go with bigger ones if you like. Your bird can't stay in the cage all the time; they naturally need to have some flight time. For this, you can get them perching bars.

They can flutter around the home and land on perches you have in various places around the house. Before you do this, you need to make sure safety is in place. You can't allow them to fly anywhere where another pet can get them. You can't have them around ceiling fans, as that can be very dangerous.

You have to bird proof your house to make sure they don't get out. Someone else in the household could walk in the door and they could fly out! This can happen in a matter of seconds. We always have a second layer of protection. We allow our African Grey Parrot to fly around in one room only. Should they get out of there, they will be inside of our home, not outside.

Try to include some regular flight time into the routine. Doing so will keep them happy and it will also provide them with plenty of exercise. That is good for their heart, lungs, to keep their wings strong, and to help them with feeling content in their environment.

Love and Trust

Some people believe only humans are capable of love. I tend to believe those who think many animal species care deeply about each other and often form strong bonds of love and trust with humans. From my own experiences, the African Grey Parrot is certainly capable of deep love and trust. They feel emotions and they can understand human emotions. You need to give your parrot unconditional love and the attention it needs. You have to build trust over time. Make sure your parrot can count on you for their basic needs and well-being. As they begin to trust you more, they will become increasingly affectionate.

You do have to be careful though, because some parrots go overboard with the love element. They can engage in jealousy! I am not kidding at all when I tell you these intelligent birds are also very empathetic. Even though our African Grey Parrot has significantly bonded with me, he picks up on the fact that my wife is sad. He often makes soft musical sounds in her presence. I think he is trying to soothe her.

There are days when I come home from work just stressed out and tense. That silly bird will start doing things that make me laugh. I think this is intentional, not just a coincidence. I firmly believe they get to know the behaviors of their owners, just like we get to learn about theirs.

It is important to realize these parrots become dependent on us for everything. They are captives rather than being able to freely explore the world and make their own decisions. Therefore, as a pet owner, you must always ensure they can trust you to offer them an environment they are happy with.

Toys and Games

Find a variety of toys and games for your bird to enjoy. Carefully select them so you don't have too many that offer them the same stimulation. Choose various levels of difficulty with them too, so they aren't always challenged to the full.

From time to time, give them something you feel is too advanced for them to complete. They may surprise you. Over time, they will do better and better with it, which proves that they have a good memory and they continually learn. It also proves that they can reason and think about how to use what they have learned and then apply it accordingly.

Keep the number of toys and games they have access to at any given point to a minimum. Don't give them free reign with them or it can be chaotic. This also makes more of a mess for you to clean up and it clutters the cages. Give them a few to interact with and then change them out when you clean the cage each time.

Quiet Time

While your parrot is going to be socializing, playing, eating, and engaging, it also needs some quiet time. As they mature, they start to carve this out for themselves more and more. With a younger bird, you may have to move the cage to a quiet location if they start to seem over stimulated.

A cage cover will also help your parrot to associate that time as being quiet time. They may still be awake under the cover but they are going to be less likely to be noisy or as active. This is a learned behavior, so when the cover is on don't walk by and talk to them or interact in any way or it will confuse them.

Clean Environment

One of their basic needs is a very clean environment. It isn't fun to clean the cage but it is a way for them to stay sanitary and to be happy. They won't drink water that is contaminated in any way. You need to make sure they always have fresh water. They may get bored and chew on the newspaper at the bottom of the cage. This is something you need to clean up right away.

Chapter 7) Buying an African Grey Parrot

I urge you to think carefully when it comes to buying an African Grey Parrot. You need to know the history of the seller and you need to get a decent price for your pet. As mentioned, it can cost between $600 and $2,000 to buy one. If you purchase one under 18 months of age, it isn't easy to tell if it is male or female.

Sometimes, the seller will have DNA testing done so they can let you know the gender. Typically, when they do so, they charge more for the females because they are able to breed. Others will get the DNA testing done at your expense if you want a specific gender.

If you don't plan to breed your parrot, then it really shouldn't matter. I suggest giving the bird a name that is neutral. You don't want to learn when the parrot gets older that it is a male with a female name or the other way around!

Species

Before you go shopping think about the price you are willing to pay and the species you want. If you don't care which gender or which species of bird you get, it opens up more possibilities for you. If you are interested specifically in the Congo African Grey or the Timneh African Grey, you need to be more selective where you buy from. They should be able to guarantee which species they are selling to you.

If they sell you a gender specific parrot, make sure that is also guaranteed. It should all be put into writing so there aren't any problems later on. If the parrot you paid a higher price for was guaranteed to be female and turns out to be a male, then you should be able to get that extra cost back from the seller. You can only enforce that if it is in writing and signed by both parties.

Never try to save money by purchasing such a pet on the black market. There is a very good chance the bird was smuggled or it was stolen. Either way, you don't want to get wrapped up in such a situation. Buy from someone you can trust.

There are several places where you can buy the African Grey Parrot. It is a good idea to explore several options before you make your decision. Find out what you can about the entity. If you see any red flags, don't buy from them. Report anything that seems suspicious and let the law investigate it further.

Where to Buy
- Private Owners
- Avian Specialty Stores
- Bird Breeders
- Bird Rescue Organizations

Private Owners

It isn't recommended to buy an African Grey Parrot from a private owner. You simply don't know enough about them. Sometimes, you will have a private owner selling young offspring due to their pair mating. They simply can't home all of them so they are looking for good homes.

This may be a good opportunity for you to buy one. I do strongly recommend you go to where the people live. Take a friend with you so you aren't alone. You just can't be too careful in today's society. Pay close attention to how the parents look and react when you examine the bird.

Spend some time getting to know the private owners and why they are selling the birds. Don't be nervous to ask them tough questions either. If you just aren't sure or you get a bad vibe, thank them for their time and leave. If they don't want to communicate with you it is best not to buy from them. They may have something to hide.

Avian Specialty Stores

Avian specialty stores are those offering exotic pets or specific types of birds. If you live in a small town, you may have to travel to the next largest city to find one. You can do a search online to find out who is out there and what they offer. You will save yourself time if you call them in advance and ask them if they have any African Grey Parrots.

If they do, you can arrange a time to go to that location. If they don't, they may be able to tell you who offers them in that area. Gaining such information can prevent you from going on a wild goose chase. This isn't the typical pet you will find in all pet stores or the mall pet location.

Always take the time to learn about any avian specialty store before you contact or visit them. Who is the owner and how long has the business been in place? Do they have any complaints against them? You need to be confident they are a legitimate business with the best practices in place.

Bird Breeders

Another option is to buy an African Grey Parrot from a bird breeder. You will have to conduct some research to find out who offers such services in your area. You have to be very selective about bird breeders though. You want to buy from someone with a solid reputation.

They need to have exceptional methods in place for mating and housing the birds. Some of them unfortunately do nothing but mate the birds as quickly as they can to make the most money. This is stressful for the birds and it isn't good for their overall health.

They may have the birds in crowded cages and they don't get the food, water, or the attention they need. It is all about getting them to reproduce. Any time you plan to buy an African Grey Parrot from a bird breeder, you need to see where the birds are kept and the conditions they are kept in.

Bird Rescue Organizations

When an African Grey Parrot is rescued, it will get the care it needs. Perhaps it is sick and needs medical care. Maybe it wasn't being fed correctly or it developed bad habits. They will do what they can to make the parrot feel well on all accounts. It won't be put up for adoption until that happens.

You may have to complete an application to get one from a bird rescue center. The process can be very rigorous. They need to be confident the bird is going to a good home. Usually, they won't approve a home where the owner has never had birds before. It is simply too risky after what the parrot has already been through.

Be honest with your application and answer all of the answers completely. Don't take it personally if they deny your request. It doesn't mean you won't make a wonderful bird owner.

It is worth your time to find out what bird rescue organizations are in your area. You can check online to find them in nearby towns too. Call and ask them if they have an African Grey Parrots. If they don't, give them your contact information. They can get in touch with you later on if they get such a bird.

Young Bird

Young birds shouldn't be separated from their mothers until they are about 12 weeks of age. Doing so younger than that isn't good for their health. They will be stressed and they won't get the care they require to do well. However, many breeders and specialty stores will advertise them for sale around 9 or 10 weeks of age.

This gives potential buyers time to check them out. It gives them a chance to secure the sale of the birds before it is time. Then when the young birds are 12 weeks old the buyers can come back for them. It is a way to reduce the time between when they can be sold and when they are actually purchased.

Adult Bird

If you buy an adult African Grey Parrot, you need to really evaluate the situation. What is going on so that the owner doesn't want it anymore? Now, this doesn't necessarily mean the parrot isn't delightful. It could be the original owner has died or is sick and no one in the family can care for it. It could be someone bought it and now realizes they can't care for it.

When it comes to re-homing these birds, there can be trust issues. It is going to take even more patience to ensure they will start to love and trust you. There is no way for you to know their fears and anxieties. You don't know what they experienced or what was lacking in their world before you came along.

They may have developed some behavioral issues you have to break. This can include screaming and biting. They may have picked up words and phrases you don't want to hear them repeating in your home. Think about all of this before you buy an adult bird.

Granted, you should be able to buy one for much less than what you would pay for a young bird. Still, you have to ask yourself how much time and energy you are really willing to put into it. The outcome can be quite rewarding or it can be a nightmare.

Before you buy an adult bird, get to know the people currently caring for it. Pay attention to how they interact with the parrot. Pay attention to the physical appearance too. You don't want to take on the responsibility for an African Grey Parrot who is sick.

Spend several hours around the bird before you decide if you will take them home with you or not. Don't be in a rush to make a decision. Don't let the other party guilt you into taking them home either. If your decision is yes, take it on your own terms.

Rescue organizations are where you will usually find adult African Grey Parrots. They may have been taken from their owners for neglect or mistreatment. They may have been taken to the rescue from an owner who just didn't feel like they could continue to take care of such a pet.

Negotiating the Price

The price ranges significantly. You can get an African Grey Parrot for about $600 but you may pay up to $2,000 for one. The younger birds tend to be sold for the highest price. Older birds may be sold for a few hundred dollars to get them a good home. They may be sold alone or with their cage and all their toys. It is a good idea to ask so you don't assume you will get something.

With a bird rescue center, you may need to pay a flat fee that is to cover part of the care the parrot received there. You may have to pay for a medical examination and for an adoption fee. The cost just depends on the African Grey Parrot you get and where you buy it from.

Ask what the price is and go from there. I love a bargain so I never pay full price for anything. Give them a counteroffer and see if they will take it. If they don't, you can give them another offer between the two price points. For example, they may say $1,000 and I will offer $800. They may say no so I offer $900.

If they are firm on their asking price you have to decide if you want the bird enough. If not, you need to keep looking. Don't pay more for one than you can reasonably afford. You don't need the financial stress!

Many pet stores and breeders will ask for a deposit on such a bird if you come in and look at it before it is old enough to go home with you. For example, if you go see the bird at 10 weeks and want to buy it, you will need to negotiate the price. Once that is decided, they may ask for $200 to hold it for you.

The money for the African Grey Parrot will be due at the time you come back to pick it up. Make sure the entire agreement is in writing and both parties have signed it. This is for your protection and to ensure the deal doesn't go sour and you lose your money.

Read all the terms and conditions of such a contract. It may state if you don't come back for the bird or you change your mind, you lose your deposit. Don't assume you will be able to get that money back if your plans change in the weeks while you wait for the bird to be old enough to go with you.

Getting your Parrot home

Unless you are buying the parrot from someone who will include the cage, you need to have some items with you when you pick it up. If you buy it from a specialty store they will have all the items you need for sale. Be prepared for your African Grey Parrot to be a bit distressed on the ride home.

Talk to it softly and make sure it has some food. Your bird may not eat or drink much for the first few days. It is going to take time for it to get accustomed to a new environment. Younger birds seem to do better with the change than older birds. However, each parrot is different based on personality and other characteristics.

Chapter 8) Living Environment & Toys

Once the decision has been made to get yourself an African Grey Parrot, you need to think about the living environment. The right conditions are essential for your pet to thrive. You have to make sure the temperature is comfortable for them. Don't place their cage too close to heating vents or air conditioning vents. This can make it too warm or too cold for them.

Cage

The cage you keep them in needs to be at least 34 inches wide and 34 inches deep. If you have a pair of birds, you want to go with a much bigger cage so they aren't crowded. You can get the largest birdcage out there if you wish, but don't go any smaller than this or your parrot may be stressed.

A great way to reduce the stress on your parrot is the location of the cage. Try to place it in a corner rather than in the center of a room. You may like the idea of it being a focal point, but it will cause stress for your pet due to the commotion around them in their living environment.

Playpen Style

I recommend also getting a playpen style of cage for your African Grey Parrot. This is a wonderful place for them to get some exercise. Keep different toys in this cage than their normal cage. Doing so will offer some different stimulation, which these birds need. The playpen style of cage also offers them a safe place to fly around and exercise.

Travel

I also recommend a small travel sized cage that is ideal for your parrot. They should have enough room in there to move around about, not too much or they will get anxious. This is perfect for when you take them to the vet because your normal cage for them will be too large. Once you place all the perches and other items in there, it can also become very heavy.

Make sure the latch on your travel cage is very secure. The last thing you want is to get your African Grey Parrot into the car but they escape when you try to take them into the vet or into the pet store.

Cage Covers

I strongly suggest getting a cage cover and using it at night. Your African Grey Parrot will soon associate the cover going on as quiet time. At first, they may make lots of noise but it won't take long for them to realize what this part of the daily routine is all about. Not only will the cover help them to have quiet time, it helps to keep them warmer through the night.

Many experts believe the cage cover can offer the bird a sense of security for the night hours. This may make all the difference between you getting a good night's sleep or being up several times a night. In my household, I have a wife, a dog, a bird, and two kids. I do all I can to ensure we can all sleep through the night!

Select a cage cover that is dark in color. This is going to encourage your parrot to sleep in later. If you are fortunate enough not to have to get up early each day, you will appreciate this. Don't substitute a towel for a proper cage cover. Terry cloth should be avoided as birds can get their toes caught in the materials.

Wash your cage cover monthly with a scent free detergent. This will help remove any signs of danger or dust. I have an extra cover so I can easily replace the one I have been using at any time.

Important Cage Details

Make sure the bar spacing on all cages is at least ¾ inch but not more than 1 inch. Perches should be placed in both types of cages. Offer several of various sizes and made from different materials. Doing so allows your parrot to exercise its legs and feet regularly.

The types of perches you can choose from include:

- Concrete perches
- Dowel perches
- Heated perches
- Rope perches
- Shower perches
- Therapeutic perches
- Wood perches

Offer your bird a variety of choices for their footing. Too many owners believe these items to be optional for African Grey Parrots. However, they can develop sores on the bottom of their feet if the stand on the same perch day after day. You definitely need a dowel perch. They also need a concrete perch to keep their nail tips from getting too sharp. Perches don't cost very much but they do offer plenty of value.

Security

Always make sure the latch on the cage is secure. It is a good idea to have a second securing mechanism on the cage. We have a small padlock on ours. More than once we came home to find our African Grey Parrot flying around the kitchen. They are very clever and they can escape a bird cage without you realizing it. This can put them in danger or result in them being killed in your absence.

Don't have a false sense of security that your bird can't fly away. Clipping the flight feathers doesn't ensure this. They are very intelligent and able to do so much with so little if they have the opportunity. Plus, those flight feathers grow back!

Avoid buying a second hand cage. You don't know if it has been damaged and repaired. It may have loose pieces your bird can swallow and become ill from or choke on. These used cages may be repainted and have toxic materials on the actual cage that make your bird ill just by breathing in those fumes.

Imported cages aren't recommended either. Some of them are still made with lead. The risk of lead poisoning can be dangerous for your entire household. It is best to stick with a brand new cage that meets all of the requirements. If you buy the African Grey Parrot from someone and they offer the cage with it, find out how old it is.

Check where it was made and other details. If you can't identify such information, you are better off replacing the cage with a new one. You don't want to take any chances when it comes to the well-being of your new pet. Ideally, buy cages made from stainless steel. They aren't going to rust and they are quite durable.

Cleaning the Cage

The bottom of the cages should be lined with newspaper. This makes it easier for you to clean up after them. Change the lining once per week to keep their living environment sanitary. You can clean one cage while they are in the other so it shouldn't ever be a problem.

Some people use wrapping paper or aluminum foil to line the cages as it is prettier than newspaper. Yet it is likely to make your parrot stressed due to the shininess and the sound of it. I don't recommend using it.

Avoid using litter for the bottom of the cage. Some people try it to avoid cleaning the cage as often but it isn't really recommended.

Never use cedar shavings either as they have irritants in them that can harm the respiratory tract of your parrot.

You can use cage tray paper, which is sold at pet shops, but it isn't cheap. Newspaper is cheap and it won't harm your pet. If they do come into contact with the newspaper, the print ink can get on their feet or their feathers. However, it isn't going to harm them.

If you start to notice odors, you may need to clean the cage more often. You will quickly learn the best timeframe for your pet. If you have a pair of African Grey Parrots, you will likely need to clean the cage every 3 days.

Never use harsh chemicals to clean it as that can be harmful to your bird. If you find stubborn urine odors or feces stains in your bird cage, you can use a citrus based cleaner or an enzyme cleaner to remove them. Don't spray the entire cage though.

Instead, saturate a cotton ball and use that to clean the area where you need it. Personally, I use white vinegar to clean the cage and it removes all odors. It also won't harm your parrot. I try to wipe up feces when I see it on the cage so it doesn't get hard and cemented.

The newspaper as lining will help to prevent urine odors and feces odors from developing in the cage. Yet if it gets on toys or on the cage, it can linger. Wipe those areas down well when you clean the cage to help keep it sanitary.

Chewing Materials

African Grey Parrots need to have access to chewing materials all the time. This ensures their beak doesn't get too long and hinder eating abilities. Offer them wood, leaves, and branches to chew on. Make sure what you give them is safe for them to chew though. It can be harmful to them if the chewing items have been sprayed with any chemicals such as pesticide or fertilizer.

Toys

Your African Grey Parrot is going to need a variety of toys for stimulation. Some of them can also be for chewing. Try to give your parrot toys that get them to use their imagination and their intelligence. There are toys that require them to perform a certain action to get a toy or to get a treat. These are fun for them to use and help them to stay well stimulated.

Don't put too many toys in the cage at one time with your parrot. Instead, rotate the toys they have access to on a regular basis. If you forget to do this, your bird will get bored with what they have access to. This can result in negative behaviors.

Examine toys each time you take them out of the cage. If they show signs of wear you need to toss them out. You don't want the bird to be able to get pieces off of them. Rope style toys last a long time but there are plenty of materials to pick from.

When you take toys out of the cage, you need to sterilize and clean them. I do this and then store them in a plastic container. Then they are ready the next time I am rotating the toys for my African Grey Parrot.

Avoid toys that have small pieces that could come off in the bird's mouth. They pose a choking hazard. Avoid those that have small bells on them too. The bells can come off in their mouths. The other risk is their beak or their toes can get stuck in the small opening of the bells.

Ladders and Swings

I love watching my parrot play on the little ladders. It offers plenty of exercise too so it is a win/win opportunity. Both the ladder and the swing mean your bird doesn't have to be on a stationary perch all the time. The ladders give your parrot a surface that is irregular, and that is a nice change for their feet.

Most of these parrots enjoy a swing in their cages. This can help them to relax and to enjoy their environment. Not all of them will use the swing, but mine always have. It is a good idea to offer it and they can choose to use it or not. A swing is also considered another perch for your bird.

You will find swings made from a variety of types of materials. I use the rope or wooden ones. There are plain swings as well as those with toys on them. You should make the swing the highest perch in the cage. Most of the time, these parrots will use that as the location where they roost over night.

I suggest you make sure you don't place food or water dishes directly under the swing or the perches for that matter. If you place them there, you will be doing far more cleaning up in the cage that you should be.

Bathing

Your African Grey Parrot enjoys drenching showers now and then. This is due to them instinctively being part of their natural habitat in the wild. Get a spray bottle and fill it with warm water. Spray/mist your parrot with it for a minute or two. This type of bathing will also help your bird to stay clean.

Not all African Grey Parrots like this at first, and they may put up a fuss. Be assured, you aren't hurting them. They will soon get used to this routine. I suggest bathing them about once a month. I usually do so on a day when I am going to change the lining in the cage. Then if the newspaper gets wet from the experience, it isn't a big deal and won't create a mess.

TV

There is a debate about exposing African Grey Parrots to TV. It can be a source of entertainment and interaction for them. You can put the TV on a timer if you are gone for an extended period of time. Just be selective about the channel you put it on or your parrot may repeat some things you aren't fond of.

Personally, I don't turn on my TV for my parrot. I have been known to leave soft music on though to help soothe it if I get the indication that my parrot is stressed about me being gone. While we have a basic routine at our house, there are times when we have to be in and out considerably more.

Chapter 9) Food and Water Basics

It is very important to offer your African Grey Parrot the right food for proper nutrition. The right food helps them to be healthy and to have energy. For younger birds, the right food helps them to grow. The amount of food they consume will vary based on age and gender.

Younger birds tend to eat less at a time but they will eat often throughout the day. Older birds will eat fewer times but eat more each time. Males tend to consume more than females. The exception to this is when the females are ready to hatch the eggs of their young. They may eat much more to help them provide the right nutrition for the process of laying the eggs.

Your parrot will also need access to fresh water. Don't assume that because there is water in their dish they aren't thirsty. If the water has been sitting there for quite some time, they will no longer touch it. If it is contaminated in any way, such as with urine or feces, they won't touch it.

Diet

The diet for African Grey Parrots in the wild consists of:

- Berries
- Fruits
- Needs
- Seeds
- Vegetation

In captivity, their diet should closely resemble what they would feed on in the wild. To give them a balanced diet you should offer:

- Dairy
- Fruits
- Grains
- Greens
- Meat
- Pellets
- Seeds
- Sprouted Seeds
- Treats
- Vegetables
- Whole grains

Balancing their dietary needs

It isn't enough to just offer your parrot a variety of foods though. Think about the food pyramid for humans for a moment. It lets us know the types of foods we should eat and the amount of them. The same is true for your African Grey Parrot. This is a good way to balance what you provide them:

- Dairy = 2% of the diet
- Fruits = 20% of the diet
- Grains = 50% of the diet
- Meats = 2% of the diet
- Seeds and nuts = 1% of the diet

- Vegetables = 25% of the diet

A poor diet is one if the main causes of serious health problems for the African Grey Parrot. They need plenty of fresh vegetables to ensure they get enough Vitamin A and carotene. Sweet potatoes and kale are highly recommended.

Pellets in the diet can help reduce the risk of Vitamin D deficiency. It will also reduce the need to add supplements to their diet on a regular basis. When possible, their vitamins and minerals need to come from food sources and not from supplements. There are times though that it isn't enough and you will need to add something extra.

Supplements

Talk to your vet about the possible need to give your parrot supplements. I don't recommend just giving them on your own. You need to know what to offer and how much to offer. However, African Grey Parrots are known to be quite vulnerable to deficiencies with Vitamin A and calcium.

A well balanced diet should reduce that risk. That isn't always the case though. Our vet has recommended we give our pet a vitamin/mineral supplemental powder. It contains:

- Calcium
- Phosphorus
- Vitamin D3

Try to ensure your parrot gets plenty of Vitamin D through sunlight exposure. If that isn't possible due to the dwelling you live in, then it may be necessary to give them a supplement with Vitamin D. It is important to find a vet that can help you customize what your particular bird needs. We will talk more about that in a future chapter.

My vet recommended adding fat to the diet of our African Grey Parrot we currently own. I give her a small amount of dry sunflower seeds each week. You can also give them safflower seeds. In the wild, palm oil is a common entity. If your parrot is plucking often, you can try this easy dietary addition and see if it reduces or eliminates the concern.

What's in the dish?

This is really, really important! African Grey Parrots, like many other birds, hull seeds. They will crack open the seeds and take the meat out of the shell. Then they leave the shell. It is similar to the way humans take off the shells of nuts and eat the insides.

Sadly, I know some people who thought their dish was full of food for their parrot. They didn't refill it and in reality, it was only full of hulls. Their bird was actually starving. It was an honest mistake but it wasn't until they contacted the vet that their parrot wasn't eating that the issue was discovered. This is concern that can so easily be overlooked if you aren't familiar with the eating habits of birds.

Overfeeding

It isn't possible to over feed your African Grey Parrot. They are going to eat what they want and the rest will be left over. Sometimes these birds get fat, so you either need to cut back on food or you need to increase exercise. My vet says you should always increase exercise and stimulation.

Your bird will get picky with food if you give them the same thing all the time. Don't give them a diet of just pellets because it is easy. They need a variety of foods. We frequently consume fresh fruits and vegetables in our household. It is easy enough to give our parrot some of them several times per week.

In general though, these birds aren't picky about eating right. They can be fussy if you get an older bird who didn't have a good diet before. It can also be hard to change the diet for your bird if you haven't been offering them what they should get on a consistent basis.

You can feed them many things you would feed your own family. Hot cereal with bananas in it is great for my kids and my parrot. They like eggs too. I often give my bird the leftovers from our dinner such as a bit of salmon and some of the vegetables.

I have seen African Grey Parrots who eat a great deal of food. I have also seen those who don't consume very much at all. Yet they thrive on both ends of the spectrum. Just like humans, there are different appetites and different metabolic rates. Your parrot may start to make a huge mess with food in the cage they don't intend to eat. If they aren't eating the food, take it out or offer them smaller portions. A lack of interaction or games to play with can result in your African Grey Parrot finding things to do for entertainment that you aren't happy with. Food all over the cage is definitely a sign you need to change the daily routine and interaction with your bird immediately.

Knowing how much your bird tends to eat on a daily basis is important. Should you notice their appetite is much less or much more than it used to be, it could be a reason to evaluate them closer. There could be a medical reason, a pregnancy, or other issue. Sometimes, it isn't anything to worry about but you do want to investigate the situation just in case.

Water

Use small dishes for water in order to keep your bird from bathing in it. The water should be for drinking only. Place it in a corner of the cage where it is less likely to get spilled than if it is in the middle of the cage. Your parrot needs access to fresh water at all times.

They will eat a meal and then drink water after they are done to help with digestion. A lack of water can result in difficult digestion for them. If the parrot continually doesn't have access to fresh water, it won't eat. They are smart enough to make the connection they need the water to help them complete the digestion process.

Change the water every morning and change it again each evening when you return home. The water should be cool and fresh. If it has been sitting there for days they will stop touching it. If there are traces of particles in the water they won't drink from it.

Dishes

Try to place the dishes for food and water in an area of the cage where they aren't likely to come into contact with urine or feces in it. Avoid areas directly under perches. When you buy a cage, it should come with dishes. However, you can also buy extras, which I recommend. They should be small in size. I have extra sets and I fill up the food and water each day in new dishes and remove the old ones.

Cleaning the dishes often helps to prevent bacteria from forming in them. These parrots can also be very picky. Even if they have water in their cage, they may not drink it if it isn't fresh. Pay close attention to the amount of food your bird eats and the amount of water they drink each day.

By learning these behaviors, you will be able to tell if there are huge changes in their diet. Eating more/less than usual or drinking more/less than usual can indicate a health concern.

To reduce the risk of health problems and digestive problems, you need to offer your African Grey Parrot a balanced diet. This will also increase the likelihood of a long life. Talk to your vet and to experts at Avian specialty shops to find the right foods for your pet that go beyond what you buy at the grocery store.

Chapter 10) Ongoing Care

By now, we have touched a great deal on just about all of the areas of the ongoing care for African Grey Parrots. However, I think it is important to put all of the pieces of the puzzle for their ongoing needs into one area for you to look at. It should be a mental inventory of what you are committing to.

Environment

These birds need an environment that is as consistent as possible. Believe it or not, they can start to figure out what will take place due to their internal clocks. I have no doubt my pet knows when I am getting up and going to work. He also knows when it is time for me to come home.

My wife and kids have a less predictable schedule due to various activities, so they come and go from the house all day long. They may go to the park on a nice day or to the grocery store another. What my African Grey Parrot has learned though is he will never be home for too long on his own.

He has learned the environment we offer for him is safe and he can trust us. That reduces so much stress and so many behavior problems. I don't think any of these birds are naughty just to do so, there is always an underlying reason connected to it.

Offer them an environment where they feel they belong. They need to be in a corner area where direct sunlight can reach the cage at various times of the day. They also need to have a temperature that is comfortable for them. We have our thermostat set at 70 and that seems to work well for all of us, including the parrot.

The environment needs to be free from risks such as other pets that can get to them, escaping from their cage, and areas around the house that could harm them such as a ceiling fan.

The environment also needs to be free of dust, dander, and mold spores. These issues can be very damaging for the lungs and overall respiratory system of your African Grey Parrot. They are very vulnerable to fungal infections if there are issues with the air quality at your residence. You certainly don't want your family or other pets breathing in such air either.

However, the way our bodies and our immune systems are, humans can tolerate much more exposure to dirty air than other pets. These birds seem to have a vulnerability to air issues far more than other types of pets. For those of you living in a humid region, there is likely mold where you live. Dehumidifiers can help to reduce the problem. Air purifiers should be in place if you own one of these birds.

Food and Water

We have already talked a great deal about offering your bird a variety of foods and plenty of fresh water. I create a menu for my African Grey Parrot each week. My wife and I make a family menu too and often we use what is on that to decide what our bird will eat. We have fresh vegetables at just about every meal, so it is easy enough to offer them to our parrot.

We always have fresh fruit in our kitchen, and we also offer that to our parrot. We buy quality pellets and other food items from the Avian specialty store not far from here. You can also buy such food items online or ask your vet to order them for you.

Make sure you know what is in any food you give your parrot. Don't assume because the product is offered it is nutritious. Take the time to read labels and to work closely with your vet to balance the diet for them. Doing so takes a bit of time at first but it sure does help them to thrive. In time, it will become very easy for you to plan food for them.

By making a menu, you can see what you have given them throughout the week. You can make sure they get foods from each group they should have. This also helps to ensure deficits don't occur due to you not realizing what they aren't getting enough of or what they are getting too much of.

Cage Cleaning

I will be the first to admit, cage cleaning is my least favorite part of owning an African Grey Parrot. I often put it off the day it is on my list of things to do, but I get it done. I never go more than 3 days without cleaning the cages. You can go a week at the most but I don't recommend it. If you wait, the dried feces will be more time consuming to remove.

You will also discover your bird thrives and is happier in a clean cage. If you start to let this go, you will notice negative changes in their behavior. It makes sense though; none of us like to live in dirty conditions. Cage cleaning is also important for the health of your family and your other pets. Bird feces usually aren't dangerous so I don't want to scare you. However, if you don't clean it up quickly, it will turn into a powder, which can float around in the air. Your bird will inhale it, your family will inhale it, and other pets can inhale it. This can irritate allergy problems or create bronchial concerns as well as serious respiratory diseases.

By keeping the cages clean, you provide the very best environment for your African Grey Parrot. You also provide a safer environment for your family and your other pets. I think we are all in agreement that is exactly what a responsible owner is going to do.

Daily Interaction

Remember, you are the flock for your parrot. If they will be home alone often, get them a mate. This doesn't mean you have to mate them per se, but they should have another bird to interact with. Still, this doesn't mean they don't need you to interact with them daily when you are home. I talk to my parrot as soon as I get up in the morning and I remove the cover from the cage.

I talk to him as I make the morning coffee. Sometimes, I read the presentation I have ready for my morning meeting. This is for me, not for the parrot, but it is still time we are interacting. I give him food and fresh water as I get food ready for the kids.

Then I go shower and get ready for work. Before I head out the door, I say goodbye to my parrot. This is a habit I always get into so he knows I am going out. He is accustomed to that routine.

When I get home from work, I greet my wife and children if they are home when I get there. Then I go in and greet my parrot. This is important so they know you are connecting with them before you go and when you get back. In the evening when my family is relaxing, I also interact with our parrot.

Before I go to bed, I tell our parrot goodnight. Then I cover the cage. This is also a routine that he is accustomed to. They learn more than words, they learn the meaning of certain words. Routine and daily interactions go a long way towards ensuring you have a very happy African Grey Parrot in your home.

Daily Exercise

On the weekends, I treat my parrot to exercise in the morning. I take him into the room with the playpen cage. He gets his workout while I exercise on the stationary bike. Daily exercise is just as important for these birds as it is for us. While I don't exercise as much as I should, my pal has the option daily.

In the evenings, our household is quiet as the kids go to bed early. My wife is usually taking care of things for a few hours around the house and I am working in my office. I take my parrot to the playpen cage during this time of the evening for an hour or so of exercise. Then I put him back in his cage while I go enjoy watching TV or talking to my wife.

It can't be stressed enough how important it is for them to get exercise every single day. They should have the option at least an hour a day. You can do it all at once or you can do so in two instalments but make sure it gets done.

Stimulation

Offering your African Grey Parrot plenty of stimulation on a regular basis is important. If they get bored, they tear things up and they become aggressive. They need toys and puzzles to keep them mentally challenged. They need to learn and they need to grow.

Stimulation for this pet is far more than what you will offer to most other types of pets. Yet it can be very rewarding as you see them learn and you see them grow. They need to be able to develop as they get older. They need to keep their minds sharp.

Training

You would never allow your child to go through life without any rules or training. Don't let that be the approach you take with your parrot. They need to have boundaries and you need to be consistent. You need to take the time to train them so they can learn and they can follow the rules.

We will talk more about training and techniques in a future chapter. If you get your African Grey Parrot when it is young, start the training early but be patient. If you get an older bird, you may find they have some bad habits you would like to break them of. This can take time, but it can be accomplished.

Preventative Care and Medical Care

We haven't covered preventative care and medical care yet, but we will do in a later chapter. This is a very important part of taking proper care of your African Grey Parrot. You need to develop a relationship with a knowledgeable vet who can assist you. Knowing signs and symptoms of various health issues ensures you know when to get help for your pet.

Costs

It is very important to understand the costs involved with this type of bird. Here is a break down of the main costs you can expect. Keep in mind the actual amounts may vary, but it will give you a good idea of what you should budget for.

- Purchase the bird - $600 to $2,000/ (£)395.34 to (£)13,178
- Main cage - $185 to $300/(£)121.9 to (£)197.67
- Playpen cage – $300 - $700/(£)197.67 to (£)461.23
- Travel cage - $50 -$100/(£)32.95 to (£)65.89
- Perches $25 - $100 each/(£)16.47 to (£)65.89
- Toys $5 to $15 each/(£)3.29 to (£)9.88
- Food $10 to $15 per week/ (£)6.59 to (£)9.88
- Vet Care $40 to $60/ (£)26.36 to (£)39.53 per check up visit, $100/(£)65.89 or more per emergency visit
- Insurance $15 to $30/(£)9.88 to (£)19.77 per month depending on coverage

Chapter 11) Possible health concerns

This chapter is so important, and the future of your pet can depend on it. If you don't take care of their health, they may be unhealthy and they may have a shortened life span. It is your responsibility as a pet owner to ensure they get the right care.

Preventative care is important. This includes offering your African Grey Parrot the best conditions for them to thrive in. A cage that is comfortable and safe reduces the risk of injuries to them by escaping. A variety of perches reduces the risk of problems with their feet.

A well balanced diet assists with proper digestion and with proper growth. It will help your parrot to have energy, to mentally be in good condition, and to be able to enjoy the environment you keep them in. Adding supplements if necessary, as approved by your vet, may be necessary to help them be as healthy as possible.

Keeping the air in your home clean is also important as part of preventative care. This includes using air purifiers, dehumidifiers, dusting often, and reducing the risk of mold in the household environment.

In spite of doing all of this, there can still be some health concerns you need to know about. Never assume your parrot will just get better. Seek health care for them when you aren't sure what is going on. Sometimes, getting proper care early makes a huge impact on the outcome.

Injuries

There can be a variety of injuries your African Grey Parrot experiences. If you notice any concerns about how they are walking or eating, you should get medical attention for them. If you notice sores, bleeding, or swelling you don't want to ignore such warning signs.

If your bird gets out of the cage, they may incur some type of injury. Any time they escape, carefully examine them. Do this for several days after you capture the bird. Signs of an injury may not show up for a couple of days. These are curious creatures and they can get hurt by a variety of items around the typical home.

Feather Picking

African Grey Parrots are more prone to the prospect of feather picking than other birds. This is often an indicator that something is off in their environment or with behaviors that must be addressed. It has to do with the bird being extremely stressed. Give them more quiet time and try to give them more of a routine to see if this helps reduce the situation.

Another reason why your bird may be engaging in such behavior is due to the feathers not being clipped or they weren't clipped correctly. You should have them clipped by a professional at a pet store or by your avian vet.

There are some over the counter medications you can get from an Avian specialty store. They are designed to reduce feather picking issues. However, they are a treatment and not a solution. You still want to find the underlying cause of the issue. Talk to your vet if the problem isn't something you are able to resolve after a few days.

Don't jump the gun though, you need to make sure it is really feather picking you are identifying. If you see lots of feathers around the cage, that may be your first reaction because you have heard about this health concern. If you bought your African Grey Parrot very young, it is going to start to go through a molting process between 8 and 10 months of age.

They are going to lose what is referred to as their baby down during this period of time. This is a natural process and nothing to worry about. Just toss out the feathers and keep the cage clean.

Respiratory Problems

There are a variety of reasons African Grey Parrots can suffer from respiratory problems. Mold, dust, or allergens in their environment are the leading causes. This is why you must have a dehumidifier if you live in an area of high humidity and you need to use air purifiers.

The respiratory system of all birds is quite sensitive, and this one is no exception. Avoid using any aerosol sprays around your bird, as it can make them very ill or kill them. Acute respiratory distress can happen suddenly. This can happen when there is some type of toxin in the air they breathe.

This can be from a product that has been sprayed in the home. Simple items including deodorant, hair spray, cleaners, or even fumes from paint can be common culprits. Exposure to such elements can cause your bird to become very ill or even die.

The symptoms will develop very rapidly, out of nowhere. If you notice any of these symptoms you need to help your bird immediately:

- Difficulty breathing
- Falls off a perch
- Lethargic
- Weakness

Get them away from the source of the issue immediately and into an area where they can have fresh air. This can clear the toxins from their airways and they will start to breath regularly again. If this doesn't happen within a few minutes, put them in the travel cage and get to the vet immediately.

Your African Grey Parrot may need oxygen therapy or fluid removed from the lungs. Bronchial openers can be used to allow the airways to widen and then oxygen can be pumped into the body. Depending on the severity of the issue, your pet may need to take antibiotics and/or anti-inflammatories for a few days to make a full recovery.

Remember that all birds are meant to fly. This helps them with improved health and reduces the risk of respiratory problems. Just make sure flight always takes place in a safe environment such as a playpen cage.

Vitamin Deficiency

African Grey Parrots are vulnerable to various vitamin deficiencies. We have touched on them a bit in the chapter about proper diet. Vitamin A, Vitamin D, and calcium deficiencies are the most common.

A lack of calcium can be due to not enough magnesium or various vitamins in the body. Such vitamins are necessary for their bodies to absorb the calcium. This is why you shouldn't just give your parrot a calcium supplement. The vet can do various tests to find out what the overall makeup of vitamins and nutrients is in the blood.

It isn't known why this species of bird needs more calcium than others. However, if they don't have enough it can cause serious health problems including seizures. The vet will often take blood work and that is how they are able to diagnose low calcium. Once that is confirmed, dietary changes and/or calcium supplements will be the treatment.

PBFD (Psittacosis and Psittacine Beak and Feather Disease)

PBFD is often referred to as parrot fever. It was first identified in 1975 by a vet in Australia. Generally, it is a flock type of disease but it can be found in individual birds that are kept as pets. As a result, the theory is it is a genetically linked issue due to some type of deficiency.

It results in feather loss and there can be some deformities of the feathers. The parrot can have thick spots of bald patches where their skin is exposed. The feather loss will continue to progress until the entire body is lacking them. The head will be the last place they fall off from.

The beak and the claws of birds with this health issue will become very brittle. They are prone to breaking and changing in shape. They can become deformed and that makes it hard to eat, to grasp, and to perch. Sadly, African Grey Parrots with this health problem will die. However, it can take many years for the issue to progress to that point.

For others, once the onset starts, the disease will progress very quickly. Often, these parrots die of other health problems due to the symptoms. For example, hypothermia, as they don't stay warm enough without their feathers to protect them.

There is still plenty of research that takes place in the USA and Australia regarding PBFD. Several studies have been completed in an effort to produce a vaccine against it but so far nothing has been evaluated to be a success.

Malnutrition

The failure to offer your parrot enough variety in their diet can result in malnutrition. Sadly, I have seen very sick African Grey Parrots at rescues. The owners didn't realize the diversity of the diet they needed. They only fed them seeds or pellets and it wasn't enough for them to thrive.

Color Changes

The only natural color changes your African Grey Parrot should develop is the red of the tail as they get older for the female genders. Otherwise, they shouldn't have changes to their coloration. If you notice such a change, it is a red flag that there is certainly something wrong with your parrot and you need to contact your vet immediately. Other causes can include:

- Feather picking
- Kidney problems
- Liver disease
- Medications
- Malnutrition

Excessive Heat

It is important to keep the temperature around 72 F for your African Grey Parrot. In the winter they need the heat and in the summer they need to keep cool. Even when you aren't home, you have to think about keeping them comfortable. An automated thermostat is the best way to do this.

However, there are times when the unthinkable happens. One day my wife came home from shopping and discovered it was very, very warm in our house. She had left the air conditioning on but it wasn't working. As a result, our African Grey Parrot was panting heavily due to the excessive heat.

This resulted in our parrot also becoming very stressed. My wife called the vet and they told her to get spray bottle and put cool water in it, then to gently mist the bird for a couple of minutes to help cool down the body temperature.

Next, my wife took the travel cage and asked the neighbor if the bird could stay there for a bit while she figured out the air conditioning. The vet did tell my wife that if the spray bottle of water didn't help in a few minutes, to bring the bird in. Luckily, it was just a bit of heat but it could have been heat stroke.

If your bird may have heat stroke, use a mild liquid soap and place the bird under a faucet offering cool water. The soap is going to help get the water underneath the features so it can actually reach the body's core. You need to make sure the water is cool, but not too cold or your parrot can then suffer from hypothermia.

Continue the water bath for about 20 minutes. Then pack your bird in cool towns around the feed and the beak. Leave these packs on when you get your parrot to the local vet clinic. They may need to give your parrot Acepromezine or Phenobarbital if it is suffering with convulsions.

Hypothermia

When your bird gets too cold, it is called hypothermia. This can occur if you leave a window open by accident and it gets too cold through the night. It can happen if the bird cage is close to an air conditioner vent. When the body of your bird gets too cold, it can lower body temperature.

Hopefully, you can take swift action to help your bird survive such a traumatic experience. Wrap your parrot in towels and blankets and hold them close to you. Don't let them move around, as you want them to generate and conserve body heat. You can use a heating pad, but never apply it directly to your pet. Instead, wrap it in a towel or two and then apply those to the bird. If you don't have a heating pad, blow warm air through a blow dryer through a towel onto the feathers. Don't blow the dryer directly on the feathers though, as the power can damage them.

Don't cover their feet but get them off any surface. Like humans, they can lose body heat through their feet. Place the bird in the palm of your hand and that will generate some heat for them. Massage one foot and then the other to help with improving circulation.

You can also place your African Grey Parrot into a pan with a few inches of warm water. Make sure the water isn't too hot or it can burn them and cause severe damages to their feet and their nerves.

64

It is a good idea to apply the heating pad and to place the feet into the warm water at the same time. To help with the warmth, take your parrot into the bathroom and turn on the shower water as hot as you can. Close the door to create steam in the bathroom. This will help ensure the air they are exposed to is also warm.

Stay Calm

I know it is easier said than done, but you need to try to stay calm when there is a health issue or an emergency with your African Grey Parrot. If you can be calm they will find safety and security in your touch and your voice. If you are a nervous wreck, it is only going to increase their level of anxiety.

First Aid Kit

I strongly suggest creating a first aid kit specifically for your African Grey Parrot. In a moment's notice, you may need to have items ready that you can use to help them. Here are the items I have in mine:

- Gauze
- Heating pad
- Hemostatic powder or gel
- Kwik – Stop (this is a cauterizing agent)
- Needle nose pliers
- Scissors

Chapter 12) Finding the Right Vet

Be very selective when it comes to the care for your African Grey Parrot. Not all vets out there are equipped to care for them. Some will give it their best shot but that isn't enough. If you don't feel right with them, you need to end the relationship. You need a vet you can create a good connection.

It is important to find an avian expert vet. If you live in a small area, you may only have one or two vets you can choose from who have the ability to care for such animals. If you aren't completely happy with them, you may have to rely on them for an emergency service.

You can travel a bit further to find the best possible avian veterinarian for routine checkups and preventative care. However, it is strongly recommended you find one vet for all the needs of your African Grey Parrot. They will be able to offer you the very best care when they know the full history of the bird. It will be easier for them to identify when something isn't right when they know how it behaves normally.

A wonderful website to help you find out your options is http://www.aav.org/search/. You can enter your country and location to find a list of possible vets. Based on what you enter, you will be able to get the name, location, and contact details for the possible vets.

If you don't have any avian vets in your area, talk to local vets to see if they offer some basic care for your type of bird. If they do, they may be able to offer you what you need to care for your African Grey Parrot. If they don't, they may be able to direct you to another vet in the area who does.

What to look for in a vet

It is important to forge a solid relationship with your vet. You need to trust them and be able to communicate with them. You need to be able to discuss the needs of your bird with them. You also need to make sure they have the right experience. Caring for a bird is different to dogs and cats, as their anatomy isn't the same.

Ask questions about the type of specialized training they have to care for your bird. It is important to work with someone armed with enough experience and information to help you create the very best environment for your African Grey Parrot. They should be able to assist you with tweaking the diet and taking care of all health concerns.

Talk to potential vets to find out how long they have been treating birds. Ask if they have experience specifically with the care of African Grey Parrots. It is best to secure a vet that does. Ask if they are a member of AAV (Association of Avian Veterinarians).

Many avian vets are also bird owners. Don't be shy to ask them about this. They can tell you if they own birds and what species. The fact that they are passionate about birds is important. Yet when they also care for one at home it means they have first-hand experience with them and that is reassuring.

Emergency Care

It is important to find a vet that offers emergency care. You can schedule an appointment to talk about your bird or for routine checkups. However, when there is an emergency, you need to be able to pick up the phone and call someone. The issue may be severe enough that it can't wait until the morning or after the weekend.

Many vets realize the importance of providing such care. Typically, they have an answering service that takes calls for them. If the issue seems important enough to warrant the vet, then the answering service will call the vet. They will either instruct you to meet them at the office or they will come to your home. Very few vets make house calls these days but some of them still offer such care.

Cost of Services

Finding an excellent vet for your African Grey Parrot is only part of the equation. You also need to find one offering decent prices for the care they provide. Ask about prices in advance so you aren't upset when you see your bill for checkups or specialized care.

Most of the time, the vet can provide you with a fee schedule. It isn't going to be exact for each visit you have. However, it can give you some general guidelines. Keep in mind your bird is considered an exotic pet and the cost of care is going to be more expensive. Emergency after hours care is also going to cost more.

Observations

When you take your African Grey Parrot to the vet, you should be at ease. The receptionist and all other staff should be friendly and professional to you. Pay attention to the way staff interact with your bird during the examination process. They should be comfortable with the bird and do all they can to put the bird at ease.

They should be able to work closely with you and tell you what you need in order to care for your bird. For example, they should have experience with the food supply for the African Grey Parrot. If you are struggling with their diet then they can help you to plan better to make sure they get all they need.

They can tell you the results of bloodwork and other testing in simple terms rather than medical terms. This allows you to get details and to be well informed about what to expect with your bird. You want to make sure you know as much as possible about their needs so you can meet them.

Routine Check Ups

Avian checkups are important for taking good care of your bird. You should schedule 1 exam annually to go over your pet's needs. The vet will weigh and measure your African Grey Parrot. They may take a blood sample so they can run some basic tests. Doing so can rule out any health concerns that don't show other symptoms until later on.

During this annual checkup they will look over the bird physically. Often, this is when trimming the feathers will occur. They may trim the nails on the toes too if you aren't comfortable doing that at home.

They will take the time to answer any questions you may have about your African Grey Parrot at that checkup. Perhaps you think your bird is eating too much or too little. Maybe you worry they weigh too much or they need more exercise.

Serious Health Conditions

It can be very upsetting when your African Grey Parrot has a serious health condition. This can be something due to the heart, lungs, liver, or kidneys not functioning like they should. The diagnosis can be hard to accept but work with your vet to evaluate the solutions.

Some serious health conditions can be resolved and your bird will get better with time and medication. For injuries, it can take time for healing to occur and you may need to have several appointments for them so the vet can see the ongoing progress being made.

The vet should share with you the various options for treatment so you can be involved in the decision of what course to follow.

They should be able to provide you with the pros and cons for each option as well as an estimated cost for the procedures.

Sharing Information

When you contact your vet due to a health problem with your African Grey Parrot, try to give them as much information as you can. Let them know about changes in their eating or drinking habits. Let them know about changes in energy levels, exercise, and the amount of talking they take part in.

If you are able to, collect a sample of urine and feces from the cage. Place them into plastic bags and seal tightly for your vet to test. If you can't collect these elements, your vet can do so at the office. Note any changes in urine or feces too, such as the frequency, consistency, or color. All of this can help your vet to determine where to start with finding out what is wrong with your parrot.

Pet Insurance

I highly recommend you invest in pet insurance for your African Grey Parrot. First of all, not all insurance plans are the same. Second, not all vets accept certain insurance plans. Take your time to shop around for the right coverage and make sure your vet can accept it.

The cost per month of such a plan is relatively low, much less than you will pay for vet visits and care for your bird. I pay my plan annually rather than monthly and I get a significant savings for doing so. My plan covers one preventative care appointment per month. It also covers a variety of emergency care needs and my co-pay is very low.

Some pet insurance plans have co-pay. This is an amount you pay each time you go to the vet. For example, it may be $25, so you pay that at each appointment. The co-pay may be more for an emergency visit. Other plans have a deductible too. This is an amount you pay out of pocket before the insurance pays anything on your behalf.

Compare various plans and what they offer for the cost. Ask questions and find what fits well into your budget. Pet insurance is a safeguard because when your African Grey Parrot is sick, you don't want to be stressed out about the cost of the veterinarian care and how you will pay for it.

Cost

The overall cost of veterinary care for your bird is important to look at. Even if you don't have insurance, you will need to pay for services. Some vets will let you make arrangements if you can't pay in full. They are more concerned with the well-being of your pet than anything else.

Yet they are in a business and if people don't pay, they can't continue that business. They may turn your account over to collections if it isn't paid in a timely manner. They may refuse to see your bird again until you have paid all outstanding payments due to them.

Communication is important if you need to make payment arrangements for the vet costs relating to your African Grey Parrot. They may ask you to sign a written agreement to pay a certain amount of money at regular intervals. They may ask you to authorize automatic payments withdrawn from a credit or debit card at regular intervals.

Find out what your choices are before you start working with any vet. If you are worried the cost of vet care can be out of your price range, you really need to not have one as a pet. It isn't fair to them to need such care but they can't get it because you can't afford it.

Chapter 13) Personality and Behaviors

Not all African Grey Parrots have the same personality. While there are typical behaviors I can share with you, each of them is unique. This is an important concept to embrace before you consider buying one as a pet. You may have fallen in love with your aunt's parrot or one you saw a few years ago at the pet store. However, that won't be your pet!

I do suggest you spend plenty of time observing and interacting with an African Grey Parrot before you buy one. Think of it as getting to know them before you decide you want to live with them. Spend a few hours at the pet store or at the breeder's to get to know a specific one. If their personality isn't what you are looking for, keep shopping.

With younger parrots, it can be hard to know what their personality will develop to be. Yet you can identify if they are shy or interactive. You can see if they are curious or not. With older birds, you have to realize they may come with some bad habits and behaviors you aren't thrilled by. Are you willing to work to change them?

Just as every person has their own personality and behaviors, that will be the case with your African Grey Parrot. Some will test your patience more than others. Some learn very quickly and others take longer to catch on to given concepts. Some talk hundreds of words and phrases while others talk very little.

I tell you all of this so you won't be disappointed and you won't feel you failed as an owner. There is plenty you can teach your parrot, yet in the end, their personality is going to shape what they do with it. If you can embrace that and not have too many expectations for the perfect African Grey Parrot, you will be doing yourself a huge favor.

What I share with you in this chapter is based on my own experiences as well as what others I am friends with have shared with me. It is also based on expert information from those who have carefully studied African Grey Parrots as pets.

Behavior Changes with Age

If you are looking for a pet because it is small and cute, will you still be interested when it grows? We see that too often people fall in love with puppy or a kitten but they don't really want a dog or a cat to take care of. Based on the long lifespan of these birds, you have to be ready for the commitment.

Your young bird is going to be curious and full of energy. As it gets older, it can be more disciplined. It can learn more words and its intelligence will grow. It is able to complete puzzles and to understand what you are saying in certain aspects. It is able to mimic sounds and behaviors it has been exposed to.

Eating habits can change as they get older. What they prefer to eat as well as how much they eat will change. Their amount of daily exercise and the types of exercise they take part in will also change. Sometimes, African Grey Parrots are very nervous when they are young. Yet as they get older, they are calmer and more relaxed as they know they are well cared for in their environment.

Some of these birds never bite but when they get several decades old they may start to if they don't know someone. They may do this as a form of defense and it is hard to fully understand. Such behavior doesn't mean they are bad or that you aren't a good owner.

Sometimes, youngsters will allow you to do things with them that they seem to enjoy. For example, they may let you hold them often. However, as they get older, they may start to show signs they don't like such behaviors as much. Pay attention to the messages they send to you.

Screaming

The idea of your African Grey Parrot screaming is a bit unsettling. I know people who were all for getting this type of pet until they learned about the screaming part of it. Flashbacks to their toddlers going through the terrible twos came to mind!

What I would like to share with you is not all of them scream. I also want to share with you that excessive screaming isn't a behavior you want to put up with. Especially if it seems to be a form of manipulation and control. These are very smart birds, but they can be manipulative at times!

If your African Grey Parrot screams every time you leave it alone, and you return, what have you just done? You have re-enforced negative behavior. That scream got them the response they wanted. If your parrot can hear you in another room but they aren't getting any attention regularly, they are going to scream to get you to notice them.

Set limits with it and make sure your bird isn't neglected in any way. As long as you do so, unruly screaming shouldn't be an issue you have to contend with on a regular basis. If it continues, you may need to incorporate various training methods until you get it under control.

There are many positive reasons why your parrot may engage in screaming now and then. Many times, they are greeting the sunrise. In the wild, when the sun comes up, the African Grey Parrots are on the go. They call out to each other from their roosting locations and they head to common feeding areas to forage for food.

This is why such birds wake up instinctively so early in the morning. I have found putting the cover over the bird cage at night is all it took to put an end to the sunrise serenading. My family treasures their sleeping time!

When your parrot is very excited, it may scream with delight! Perhaps it is happy to see you when you walk in the door. It may have figured out a puzzle it was working on. They may be playing with you or playing with a new toy and they let out a high pitched scream that lasts just a few seconds. Don't reprimand them for doing so.

These parrots eat lots of foods you typically consume too. Don't eat in front of them and expect them not to scream. My African Grey Parrot loves bananas. If I am walking in the room with one, he is going to let out a loud scream. He is protesting that I have something he wants. Remember, they see us as part of their flock and they want to share what you have.

If you give them a bit of what you have, they will be content. If you aren't willing to share, simply don't eat in front of them. I tend to share because I am often eating snacks as a walk around the house taking care of various chores. I don't think it is a big deal to give my pet a few bites of what I have – as long as that food item is part of their approved diet.

Greetings

These parrots often scream when you walk in the door and when you are leaving. This can make you uneasy, thinking that they are screaming all day long. It can make you think they continue to scream long after you are gone.

There is a very good chance they are just using such a call as part of their greeting for you – their flock. It is important to establish routine, so tell your parrot goodbye when you leave and hello when you return. This is going to reduce separation anxiety and it is also going to reduce the tendency for them to scream long after you go or for a long period of time before you return.

If you are curious about the duration of the screaming, set a voice activated tape recorder close to the cage as you say goodbye and leave. You are likely going to find out the screaming ends soon after you walk out the door. It likely starts again as they hear you approach the door to walk in. They aren't just screaming all day long in your absence.

Warnings or health issues can also be reasons why your African Grey Parrot is screaming. There may be something alarming around that they aren't used to. Once, a friend had a parrot doing this for a few days. They later found a snake in the same room! They think the screaming was a warning that there was something else in there that shouldn't have been.

Your bird is obviously stressed if the screams are accompanied by a body that is very stiff and upright. You need to do all you can to calm your parrot and to find out what has it feeling so threatened. It won't be calm until it feels a sense of security again.

The screams may be an early indicator that something is wrong with your parrot regarding health. They may have an injury or an illness that causes them pain and discomfort. If you can't seem to identify what is causing the distress screams, it is time to make an appointment with the vet for further evaluation.

Favoritism

I have touched on this a bit, but be ready for favoritism as the owner of an African Grey Parrot. Typically, they will attach themselves to one person in the household. This is the person they often interact with the most. Now, our bird was with me for several years before my wife entered the picture. Then the kids came along.

While he does well with all of us, he certainly favors me. I am not the one home the most but I am the one he interacts with the most. I feed him, clean the cage, and train him. My wife does check on him throughout the day and give him fresh water. He is fond of the rest of the family but the affection and the interaction isn't the same.

This can create some hard feelings in your household. Don't fight over the attention of your parrot. They are going to choose who they bond with based on instinct and trust factors. It really isn't a contest and it isn't about you but rather about them feeling comfortable.

My mom is afraid of birds, which is funny I think, but my parrot can always tell mom is nervous. That makes our parrot nervous, so of course he isn't going to interact with her well. She will talk to him and he will never respond. Even though I know he knows the words she is saying, he is silent. I can say the same thing to him a moment after she walks out there door and he will say them.

It is about controlling his environment and I can't deny that. I would never discipline my bird for not interacting with others the way he does with me. Not every owner realizes this is part of their personality and part of their normal behaviors. They become embarrassed when their bird doesn't interact well with everyone that comes over.

Chapter 14) Teaching them to talk and interact with you

This is a fun chapter, and one I am sure you will enjoy. Part of the perks of having such a bird is the fact they can talk. Yet you need to teach them how to do so and you will find they pick up plenty just hearing sounds all around you. Soon, they will be interacting with you all the time.

You may find your parrot is far more vocal than you bargained for. They love to talk and to hear sounds. You may find joy in hearing them mimic someone in your household or something you heard on the TV. It is an exciting time and you can be playful with the teaching.

Don't have unrealistic expectations with your African Grey Parrot when it comes to teaching them to talk and interact with you. They shouldn't be considered your best friend. You shouldn't be telling them your deepest secrets or your PIN for your bank ATM card.

Teaching your African Grey Parrot to talk and interact with you is much like teaching a toddler to talk. They often have a short attention span and you should reward them when they do well. Don't force learning on them, but make it something they look forward to.

It is a slow paced journey with short words at first. Then you can build up to phrases and sentences. Since each parrot is different, the speed of learning can also be different. Don't compare your success to that of another owner or you will become frustrated and feel like you failed. It isn't a competition!

When you first get your parrot, the priority should be for them to feel comfortable in their new surroundings. Don't try to teach them to talk on the ride home! They are going to be stressed and they are going to need some time to relax and to trust you. They may not say anything for quite some time until they know this is their home and what to expect from you.

Never raise your voice to your parrot or your will isolate them from interacting with you. They are going to feel threatened and it isn't something they will soon forget. They always need to know the environment is a good one for them, where they have freedom to express who they are and what they need will be provided for them.

As they start to settle into the new environment, they will relax. You will notice they eat better and they are active. It is then you can start to work with them. Remember, they will only remember bits and pieces at a time. Some birds are ready to learn around 6 months of age. Others aren't ready until they are fully mature around 18 months.

Introduce words as you feed them and say "lunch" or "drink your water my love" so they get to know your voice. Talk to them when you introduce new toys or games to them. They love to hear you talk to them and it will help them to feel encouraged to start talking to you too.

Watch what you say

Birds are much like little ears of children, they also pick up what we don't want them to say! Be careful talking about things you don't want them to say. I was appalled once when my parrot mimicked a stupid fight I had on the phone with an insurance guy!

Avoid profanity if you don't want your parrot to pick it up. Between watching what we say around the kids and the bird, my wife and I are pretty much profanity free these days!

Don't tell your bird you hate your in-laws or you don't want to go to a party your spouse is dragging you to. I am warning you now these issues tend to come back to haunt you in the worst possible way.

If others come to visit, you need to watch what they say and how they interact with your African Grey Parrot. You don't want them to intentionally teach your parrot something bad because they think it is funny.

Often, visitors assume a parrot is going to copy what they say but that isn't the case. If they don't know that person they will likely not do so. This is important for you to know so you don't try to coax them or reprimand them. You don't want to make it a big deal.

If the parrot wants to talk while others are around, so be it. Some of them love to be the center of attention and they will talk and talk. In fact, they may talk loudly to try to be louder than the conversation you are having with that person. Others are shy and they are going to clam up when people they aren't used to are around.

Exposure

A great deal of teaching your parrot to speak is going to be exposing them. This can be you just talking to them or even singing to them. You can talk to your family around them or talk on the phone. Turn the TV on so they can hear it or the radio.

One of the tricks I used was playing an audio book on my computer while I was gone. Some of those books are hours long, and my parrot was able to listen to it in my absence. I think he learned plenty from that, and it was something fun for me to share too.

If you have a pair of parrots, you do need to be careful. You don't want them to develop their own lingo that the two of them share but you are clueless about.

If you decided to get a second, make sure the first has learned plenty of words first. This will make it easier for them to continue to learn when the new bird joins them. It will also encourage them to teach the second bird words, so the process will be easier for you than it was the first time around.

There are so many words out there you can use to interact with your African Grey Parrot. By talking to them and using other tools, you will find their vocabulary can quickly expand. It isn't uncommon for some of them to know over 1,000 words. Yet they can understand the meaning of far more than that.

Once of the perks of getting a younger parrot is you get to see them go through this amazing transformation. You get to be part of their journey of not saying a word to picking up a few words to talking in sentences. It is unlike anything you have ever experienced!

Chapter 15) Training Techniques

Don't be lazy when it comes to training your parrot! I see this all the time and then owners are disappointed. They wish their African Grey Parrot would do this or do that. They wish it wouldn't engage in this behavior or that one. The truth is, they only have themselves to blame. They didn't take the time to train their pet and now they have to live with those consequences.

The types of training techniques you use for your African Grey Parrot are up to you. Take the time to explore different choices and decide what you are happy with. You need to be very comfortable with the training methods before you can incorporate them with your parrot.

These are very intuitive birds, and they will know if you are nervous or unsure of yourself. This is going to make them nervous and not interested in the training. Then you set both of you up to fail from the very start. Go through training methods on your own a few times before you present anything to your parrot.

However, you need to be consistent so they can learn and they know what to expect. If you find one method isn't working well, try another but do give it some time. Progress is going to be slow rather than all at once. You must be patient and you need to train on a regular basis.

Always think about where you started because when you do feel like it isn't moving along well, you can see how much they have grown and learned. Take videos now and then of the training sessions too. This is a good method for you use to see what you are doing well and what your bird is doing well.

I have done the videos because I get so caught up in the learning I don't realize my tones or my expressions. By playing back the videos, I was able to see what I was doing that wasn't working.

Yet I was also able to gain plenty of confidence with what was doing well and that encouraged me to continue with the training.

Short Sessions

The attention span of your parrot for training is going to be very short. Keep the sessions to about 20 minutes. More than that is just a waste of your time and it can cause stress for your bird. Build on what you have taught them through reviews and challenges.

Learn about the best time of day or night to train your parrot. Some of them are bright and alert in the morning and that is the best time to work with them. Others are too excited in the morning, so working with them later in the day is a better alternative.

The personality of your parrot has to be considered too. Some are people pleasers and others are very stubborn. Don't fight it but rather incorporate it in the learning. For those that like to please, always give tons and tons of encouragement. For those that are stubborn, you have to make it seem like you don't really care if they learn or not. Spin it so they want to do it, not so they think you want them to do it!

Positive Reinforcement

You will find your parrot wants to please you. Positive reinforcement is going to encourage them to continue working on what you try to teach them. You always want to reward them for their efforts. This should be through praise and small treats. If you make the training enjoyable, they are going to do better for you.

If you are a patient individual, this won't be too hard for you. If you are demanding and fast paced, it can be harder for you to back off and just go with it. I think training my bird helped me to be more relaxed and to just take things as they come. At first, I had this agenda that just really didn't work.

Puzzles and Games

The learning should always be fun, so find various puzzles and games. There are products out there made specifically for birds. These interactive options allow you to really teach them while they think you are just socializing and playing a game.

Toys should always be safe for your bird to have. Avoid those with small pieces that can come off in their beak and cause choking. Carefully inspect the toys when you clean the cage.

Find toys at avian shops, your avian vet office, and online that are specifically created to stimulate parrots. Don't give your bird the same toys you give to your dog or your cat!

Obtain toys of various learning levels so your bird can have it easy with some learning and be very challenged with other learning. Mix and match the toys they have access to on a regular basis. This will prevent them from getting bored.

Toys should always be kept clean and sanitary. Store them in plastic bags after you clean them. If you notice any signs of strain or tears, you should toss them out. This is especially true with rope toys. If you see any fraying, toss them out because the small strains could come off in your parrot's mouth.

Tricks

There are plenty of tricks you can teach your African Grey Parrot. Start out with simple tricks and then work up to more complex ones as they are stimulated to do so. Only teach them one trick at a time so they don't get confused.

Keep in mind teaching your parrot tricks isn't about showing off or making them a prime act when you have guests over. It should be about stimulating them and keeping them happy. It should be about the two of you interacting and building your bond.

Start out with some very easy tricks and build from there. As your parrot learns some simple tricks, it will boost their self-esteem with it. They will love the praise they get from you. At the same time, it will boost your self-esteem and encourage you to continue to try new tricks with them. I am a visual learner, so watching videos about tricks has helped me.

After watching videos a few times, I would be able to go work with my parrot the right way. It was important for me to feel in control and to show that I was confident in what I was asking them to do. I don't recommend you try tricks with your bird until trust has been established.

When to start

It is recommended to start training your parrot at a young age. Keep in mind that they aren't going to be ready for complex learning yet. However, if you don't teach them correct behaviors at a young age, you will have to correct their bad habits later on.

The amount of time it will take for trust to be in place depends on the environment and the connection between you and your African Grey Parrot. You will notice it starts to build over time. Ease into introducing a trick and if they don't respond well you may need to wait.

Consistency

Even though your life is busy, make the training a consistent part of the routine. Your bird will respond better when you do. They will become familiar with your body language, your voice, and your preferences for their behavior. Be consistent about what you want them to do and how to do it. Don't let bad behaviors slide tonight and then reprimand them for it in the morning. That will only confuse your African Grey Parrot.

You will find the parrot starts to follow the behaviors you are encouraging because they know it pleases you. They want your attention and realize when they do what you ask, they get it. Ignoring your parrot when it engages in bad behavior is a very effective way to teach it what is accepted and what isn't.

Simple Commands

As you teach your parrot to follow instructions or to perform tricks, you need to teach them simple commands. They will quickly understand that what you are saying means a particular thing. During the teaching phase, mimic what you would like them to do when you say the command.

Step up is an important command, as your parrot will learn to step onto your fingers. As you say "step up" put your finger out for it to settle on. Give him or her praise for doing so. You can also use this command to get them to step onto a given perch. They will understand the command and if you don't have your finger out, they will realize they need to go to the perch instead.

Step down is the next command, so they know to go from your finger back into the cage. When the step up, leave the cage door open so they can associate going back inside. If they don't do this on their own, stay "step down" and place the parrot from your finger back into the cage. You can also use this command to get them to step down from a given perch.

The call to your bird for them to give you their attention is important. I say "come" in a firm voice for my parrot. I know some people who whistle or use a different word. It doesn't matter – but pick something and be consistent with it. You should also use the same phrase for when you are leaving such as "see you soon" or "be right back" and they will associate that with you being away for a period of time.

Training Videos and Courses

You may be saying you really have no idea where to start teaching your African Grey Parrot. Don't worry, you don't have to figure it out on your own. There are plenty of training videos on the Internet. They can show you step by step how to complete a particular trick or type of behavioral training.

There are also complete courses that offer you a variety of options. This can be fun because you can use the tool at your own pace. You can view the materials for a lesson and then incorporate them with your parrot. You can stay on the same lesson as long as you need to before you move on. Don't be in a hurry to start a new lesson if they don't have a firm grasp on the current one.

Training Mistakes

Training your African Grey Parrot can be fun but it takes time and patience. If you do it incorrectly, you are going to be frustrated and disappointed. Your parrot is going to be stressed and frustrated too. There are some training mistakes you need to avoid making.

Never force your parrot to take part in the training. If they are losing interest early in the session, let them be. Try it again later when you have their full attention. Never yell at your parrot for making a mistake or not listening. Don't withhold food or water from them either.

Don't let your parrot get into bad habits from the start. You may think it is cute how they nibble on your finger. The problem though is as your bird gets older, they think it is OK to do so. Soon, that nibble will become a full blown bite and you don't want that to happen. Nip such behaviors in the bud from the start so they don't become an issue later on.

These birds love to be dominant, to be in control. Make sure you don't let that happen. They need to know you are in control and you will care for them. If you appear to be intimidated, they are going to feel those emotions. Don't fall into the trap of reinforcing negative behaviors either. For example, don't cater to them when they scream or they act aggressively.

Chapter 16) Potential Behavioral Problems and Solutions

I wish I could say it is all fun and games with this type of pet. Yet I want you to go into this with your eyes wide open. Otherwise, you are going to regret it and that isn't helping you or your bird. I have seen people give up on their bird due to behavioral problems. In reality, it wasn't the bird trying to be bad and it wasn't that the owner didn't care about them.

It was all about miscommunication. We all know that can occur with people in relationships. It can happen with you and your partner, with family, with friends, and even with people you work with. Your African Grey Parrot can't talk to you in a way that involves a back and forth conversation.

They can't convey to you in spoken words about any unmet needs they have or anxiety. Yet the underlying causes of behavioral problems such things and you have to be willing to listen so the concerns can be resolved.

Nothing will make you regret getting an African Grey Parrot for a pet like dealing with ongoing behavioral problems. Keep in mind that as the owner, you have to set the boundaries. This is easier to do when you get the bird when it is young. Older birds may not have been well cared for or they may have behaviors you don't like but the previous owner didn't mind.

It is important to understand that behavioral problems with these parrots are often the result of something not being right in their environment. They love to know they are pleasing you and therefore they will engage in behaviors that you praise them for. When they start doing other behaviors, it isn't because they are trying to be naughty. It may be the only way they know to cope with a given scenario.

Nervous Behavior

Each African Grey Parrot has their own personality. Some are quite timid and shy while others are more outgoing. Nervous behaviors are more common in those who are timid. In fact, many potential owners spending time with birds before they buy one will bypass those who seem too timid.

As a parrot gets comfortable in the home you have created, the nervousness should be reduced. Younger birds tend to outgrow this as they get older. When you bring home an older bird, try to remember that everything they are familiar with has just changed around them. They are going to be nervous until they start to trust you and become familiar with the new surroundings.

You can help to reduce nervous behaviors by being very patient with your African Grey Parrot. Never force it to engage with you or to sit on your finger. Let the bird gain confidence by knowing he or she can go into the cage and retreat to a private time if they wish. Always talk encouragingly to your parrot in a tender voice. This type of positive reinforcement will encourage good behaviors.

Phobia

Believe it or not, some African Grey Parrots develop a phobia of something. It could be a particular person, smell, or sound. A phobia is an irrational and persistent fear of something. Pay attention to what could trigger such behaviors. Do what you can to increase their level of comfort. It may be you have to limit the use of certain smells around the bird. You may have to limit certain types of music or sounds.

When your parrot has a phobia, they will give off body language to indicate they aren't comfortable with the current circumstances around them. They may become very rigid or they may scream.

Feather Picking

When they are nervous, frustrated, or bored, feather picking can occur. Sometimes, there are medical reasons for this, as mentioned in a previous chapter, so you should talk with your vet. If a medical cause isn't found, try to offer more interaction and stimulation for your parrot on a daily basis.

The toys your parrot has may need to be replaced or rotated. Perhaps they are ready for more challenging training or more challenging games. They may not be getting as much of your attention as they used to. If that is the case, make it a point to spend more time with your African Grey Parrot each morning and evening.

Change of Environment

Change can result in some birds not eating or becoming aggressive. These parrots don't like change. Adding a new pet or a new baby to the household can upset them. A change in your work schedule can be difficult for them to adjust to. I know when I work out of town our parrot doesn't do so well with it. Moving to a new home or even taking the bird to the vet can all be a change they aren't happy with.

Be patient with them and do all you can to encourage them to get to know the new surroundings. Talk to them, give them their favorite toys, and give them their favorite foods during the change. Spend more time with them so they that trust whatever is taking place they are still going to be OK.

Biting

You certainly don't want to allow your parrot to get into the habit of biting as a youngster. As they get older, that beak gets stronger and it is going to hurt! Identifying what is a bite and what is touching is important. If the skin is just red, they were trying touch or to taste. If there is a pinching sensation, that is a nip. If there is either bleeding or bruising, it is considered a bite.

Typically, biting occurs due to youngsters being curious about their surroundings. Teach them early on that such playing isn't acceptable and it should take care of the issue. As your bird gets older, biting can be an indicator they aren't tolerating behaviors. Even if they once did, those behaviors may now bother them.

For example, they may tire easily of being held. If a person continues to do so, biting may be the last resort. Your parrot may instinctively feel that they haven't been able to get away from the person by making noise or squirming so they are going to bite and see if that releases them.

Pay attention to the signals you get from your African Grey Parrot. If they are getting anxious, allow them to go back into their cage. Don't let visitors force your pet to play and interact with them. They are more likely to bite those they don't know than someone they trust.

Expert Help

Don't feel like you have failed or you shouldn't have this type of pet if you aren't getting to the core of the behavioral concerns. When you have tried to make some changes but they aren't working, it is time to look into expert help and opinions.

Start by making an appointment with your vet. Talk to them about the changes in behavior and what you have done to try to resolve them. They may suggest you change the exercise routine or the diet you have them on. If that doesn't help, they can also do some tests such as blood work to rule out any medical reasons for the behavior.

You can search online for books, videos, and training programs to help you get your African Grey Parrot to stop engaging in certain types of behaviors. Follow the steps they offer and you should start to see some improvements. Yet since every bird is different, it may not always go as quickly as you think it should or work out as planned.

You may have to try several solutions to find one that really does work. You may have to try several methods because symptoms can sometimes overlap and you aren't 100% sure which problem area the concern falls into.

There are some professionals in the avian field you can connect with and they will actually come to your home. They will evaluate your parrot and they will watch how you interact with them. Based on that information, they will give you a plan of action to get your bird to change behavior. It may take them several days or weeks accomplish this.

Getting someone to come to your home to work with your bird should be a last resort. This is going to be a very expensive endeavor, so do all you can to resolve the problem on your own. Don't give up on your pet because that isn't going to teach them and you will feel guilty if you get rid of them.

You will also feel frustrated and angry if you allow them to continue with those behaviors. Take action and identify the problem for what it is. Stay logical and don't let your emotions get the best of you. It may be a rough time for you and your parrot but if you stick with it, you will get through it.

Chapter 17) Common Mistakes to Avoid

Don't dwell on what could go wrong with this type of pet, focus on what it will be like when it all falls into place. Every owner and every African Grey Parrot are different and unique. How a pair will mesh and enjoy the company of each other is up to them to decide. I know the relationship I have had with each of my parrots has been very different.

Being prepared to be an owner of such a pet is the important thing. With awareness comes the ability to prevent serious health risks or injuries. It can help you to prevent behavioral problems and to have confidence as an owner.

In this chapter, I just want to share with you some common mistakes to avoid. Try to make your experience with your parrot as positive as it can be. Spend time with them, feed them, keep the cage clean, and work with a qualified vet. These are the main points that will ensure a healthy lifestyle for your parrot. You don't have to feel guilty when you know those needs are being met consistently.

Black Market Purchase

It may be tempting to buy such a bird on the black market. You can get them for much less than at a pet store. Yet you don't know if that bird was smuggled into the country illegally. You don't know if it has health problems. The bird may have been stolen from someone's home during a break in. That may seem outlandish, but it does happen.

It is very cruel that someone would steal a bird like this from a home just to resell it. Yet it happens because of the amount of money that can be made by doing so. They don't care about anything other than lining their own pockets with some cash in a hurry.

Showing Off

I will admit, I have been guilty of this one, but that doesn't mean it wasn't a mistake. Don't show off with your parrot for others. Don't ask it to say this or to do that. It will make them nervous most of the time.

Don't buy an African Grey Parrot either for the sole purpose of trying to have some bragging rights. Your friends and family may be impressed for a short period of time that you have a talking bird. Yet you are the one responsible for its care and you need to make sure you are onboard with this for the right reasons.

Not Securing a Vet from the Start

Don't wait until your bird needs a vet in a hurry and then you are frantically calling to find one. You need to secure one from the start. They need to evaluate your bird at least once a year. Don't avoid taking them in and only do so when they are ill or injured. Build a lasting relationship with that vet.

Being Lazy with their Diet

If you have read the dietary information thoroughly, you realize the value of offering them plenty of types of food. Yet I know people who will still say it is easier to just feed them seed and pellets. Again, if you aren't going to put 100% into their care, then don't get such a bird!

Not Cleaning the Cage

Don't make excuses for cleaning the cage. Once you get the hang of it, this will only take you about 15 minutes to complete. A week is the longest stretch of time you should go between cleanings. If your bird uses the bathroom often, then you need to clean it every couple of days.

Not Thinking Long Term

You may be all for getting this bird today, but how will your life be in 5 years? Will you be going off to college or do you want to join the military? If so, such a pet isn't going to work well with that new direction in your life. Down the road, you will likely get married and maybe have children. Will you still want to take care of your parrot then?

As your bird gets older, the health care becomes even more important. Are you going to stay committed to providing such care with a qualified vet? In reality, my young children may be grown and have children of their own while my African Grey Parrot is still thriving in my home. I definitely am committed to keeping him around and caring for him. Just make sure you realize it is a long term commitment – much longer than with most other pets.

Depending on your Parrot

While you should interact daily with your African Grey Parrot, don't become too dependent on them. If you are depressed or withdrawn from the rest of the world, it can be too easy to do. You spend all your time with your parrot and it is like you always have someone to talk to. They are your pet, your companion, and that means something important.

Yet you need to forge solid relationships with family and friends. You need to focus on work and your hobbies. Don't let your parrot become the center of your entire universe. Don't feel guilty about going to work or going out to have fun. Set boundaries with your time with them so they don't become too dependent on you either.

Failure to Stimulate your Bird

The intelligence of the African Grey Parrot means it continually needs to be stimulated and challenged. There is no shortage of games, toys, puzzles, and learning activities out there for them. It is up to you to buy them, to incorporate them, and to rotate them.

Not Having Fun

What good is it to have any type of pet if we don't have a good time with it? Sure they are work but that is all worth it for the fun times and the bonding. Let go of the stress and the doubts and give yourself some rewards for your efforts. It is a learning experience to become a great bird owner.

Conclusion

Are you ready to buy your African Grey Parrot? You may be very excited about that prospect. Hopefully you read all of the chapters and you know what you are up against. Yet it hasn't deterred you from going the distance, so you can enjoy this wonderful pet.

If you have decided this pet isn't right for you, don't feel guilty about it. Being well informed and making a decision based on what you know and your lifestyle habits is important. It shows a great deal of maturity and responsibility. Perhaps in the future getting one as a pet will be the right move for you.

I would much rather see a person wait or dismiss the idea completely than to get an African Grey Parrot and be overwhelmed with it or neglect it. On a side note, if you do get such a bird and you find you can't care for it, find a wonderful home for it. Talk to your local pet store, your vet, and even a bird rescue location to see if they can help you to re-home your parrot.

However, if you do feel right now is the best time for you to get one, go for it! You are armed with the information you need to get your bird and to successfully care for it. You know it isn't all going to be rainbows but you are willing to go through the rough spots to have this amazing pet in your life. I will tell you from experience that having an African Grey Parrot is either going to be one of your prized possessions or it is going to be the worst decision you ever made. It all comes down to how this bird is raised and cared for. Set limits through positive reinforcement.

Every African Grey Parrot has certain behaviors that are genetic and part of their personality. Yet I firmly believe you can encourage them and shape them into being respectful and to follow the limits you have set. Don't make excuses when they say bad words or when they scream without it being a medical need.

Show them you are the leader of the flock and they need to show you respect.

Instinctively, they aren't known to enjoy touching all the time. You may be able to cuddle it now and then for a brief period of time. They may not do well around small children or other pets. You really have to think about your environment now and into the future with such a bird.

When things do change such as bringing home another pet, a baby in the household, or moving, you need to do all you can to make sure your African Grey Parrot is calm and relaxed. Your presence, talking to them, and giving them their favorite toy will all help with the change.

Give them ample time to get used to their new home. Don't push them to interact during that period of time. They will get back to their routine habits when they are ready. Encourage them, spend extra time with them, and try to make the changes less stressful.

Pay close attention to the dietary needs of your bird. If you feed them a balanced diet, they are less likely to suffer from serious health issues. Sometimes, health concerns are genetic in nature and can't be avoided. Even well cared for parrots sometimes get injured or become ill.

They will all eat different amounts of food, but make sure you have plenty for them when they are hungry. Fresh water all the time is important so they don't become dehydrated. Remove uneaten food from the cage so they don't use it to make a mess.

If you are very familiar with their normal behaviors and appearance, it is going to be easy for you to see the onset of symptoms that indicate something isn't right. Work with a vet in the area with experience in avian care. Get to know them and their practices so you can rely on them for checkups as well as emergency services.

These birds love to see their owner. Praise your bird often, from the time it is a youngster, and even when it is a fully grown adult. They will continue the behaviors you encourage, so that is why you can't cater to them when they scream for you or other negative behaviors.

It can be tough, but if you realize the bigger picture you will be able to stay strong when you need to with such discipline and rules. Take the time to learn various training techniques you can incorporate with your parrot. You may need to experiment to find what works the best for you both.

Rely on training manuals, books, and videos to help you get through the difficult times. There is more than one way to raise a happy and healthy parrot though, so don't feel overwhelmed. Read the materials out there and then implement what you agree with and what works well for you. It may be necessary to try several methods before you find something both you and your parrot can use as common ground.

Encourage a variety of types of learning including new words, solving puzzles, and interacting with you. Teach your African Grey Parrot basic commands so he or she can follow instructions. Identify negative behaviors and do your best to eliminate them as soon as you can. The longer they are allowed to continue, the harder it is to correct them.

Only buy your parrot from someone with a great reputation. Take your time to look around and make sure the bird is one with a personality you are going to take a liking to. Your goal should be to provide an environment that always makes your parrot as happy as possible.

By raising your bird correctly from the start, you reduce the risk of behavioral problems and serious health concerns. Continue to learn about your parrot through online forums, videos, books, and experts. Work with avian experts in your area including those at resource centers, pet stores, and veterinarian offices. It may be a huge responsibility but it is also going to be something so rewarding that it is beyond words.

Remember that each of these birds is unique in what they offer and what they are all about. Their level of intelligence and their ability to learn is phenomenal but not all of them are interested in doing so. Accept the personality of your parrot for what it is. You can encourage them but you can't force them and a good owner knows where to draw that line.

You need to know their limits and you need to be honest with yourself. Why are you so interested in them doing something in particular? If they don't want to learn a given song or trick then try something new. You will find they learn easier when they are passionate about what is taking place.

Always continue to interact with your parrot over time. The novelty of them in your life is going to wear off. Yet it should be replaced with feelings of being in awe of them and loving them. There will soon come a time when you wonder what you ever did without them in your life. With such an exceptional lifespan, they are going to share so much with you if you let them!

Without a doubt, the African Grey Parrot takes time and quality care in order to thrive as a pet. If you are capable of doing that, you will be grandly rewarded with a pet that loves you and trusts you. It is a remarkable bond that you will forever be grateful you had the opportunity to experience.

Resources

www.birdchannel.com
www.all-pet-birds.com
www.aav.org
www.anafricangreay.ca
www.lafeber.com
www.goodbirdinc.com
www.animal-world.com
www.africangreyparrots.net
www.theparrotsocietyuk.org

Printed in Great Britain
by Amazon